MICHAEL
OWEN

World Cup Heroes:

MICHAEL OWEN

Oliver Derbyshire

JOHN BLAKE

Published by John Blake Publishing Ltd,
3 Bramber Court, 2 Bramber Road,
London W14 9PB, England

www.johnblakepublishing.co.uk

This edition published in paperback in 2010

ISBN: 978 1 84358 179 6

British Library Cataloguing-in-Publication Data:

A catalogue record for this book is available from the British Library.

Design by www.envydesign.co.uk

Printed in Great Britain by CPI Bookmarque, Croydon CR0 4TD

1 3 5 7 9 10 8 6 4 2

Papers used by John Blake Publishing are natural, recyclable products
made from wood grown in sustainable forests. The manufacturing processes
conform to the environmental regulations of the country of origin.

1

Michael Owen was born in England, at 10.20 pm in the Countess of Cheshire Hospital on 14 December 1979, weighing 7 pounds 15 ounces (3.6 kilograms), to English parents, Terry and Janette Owen. He was the fourth of five children: two elder brothers, Terry and Andy, an elder sister, Karen, and a younger sister, Lesley.

He went to school in Wales and played football for Deeside Schools and Flintshire Schoolboys, both representational teams in northeastern Wales. He once had a trial for Wales Schoolboys but never played for them and would never have qualified to play a full international for Wales. Michael Owen is English.

As Owen told the *Western Mail*, 'I've spent virtually my entire life in Wales so there's something Welsh inside me, although it's not blood.'

Owen's dad played professional football for nearly 15 years from 1966 to 1981. A striker like his son but far less prolific, Terry scored seventy goals in 299 league games during a career that took him all across England. But Terry Owen was never one to brag about his time as a footballer, and didn't advertise the fact by adorning the family home with shirts or team photos from his playing days. When Michael was growing up he didn't even realise his father had played professionally until his big brothers told him.

As far as young Michael was concerned, the most significant clubs his dad played for were Chester and Everton – Chester because this was where Owen Sr had been happiest as a footballer and thus where he decided to settle with his young family when his playing days were over; and Everton because they were the team Owen Jr supported, since they still gave his dad match tickets.

Michael was never pressured into anything by his father. Terry would just do everything to make sure his son had the best shot at being a footballer. And, although Owen Sr never said anything to his son, he did tell some friends that Michael would play for England one day, and the sensible ones among them made some money out of the bookies from it.

A natural sportsman, Michael Owen was good at whatever he turned his hand to: athletics, with a personal best of 11.4 seconds over 100 metres as a young sprinter; rugby, using his pace to score many tries from centre; cricket, where he was captain of Hawarden Under-16s, opening the bowling and batting with a top score of ninety-two; snooker, with a top break of sixty-four; and even boxing.

'I boxed for a few years. I wasn't bad – but I certainly prefer goal-scoring to boxing,' Owen recalled in the *News of the World*. 'It was really scary. I always played football and was used to having 10 team-mates around me to help. But now suddenly I was in there on my own, facing someone

who wanted to give me a real pasting. I won both of my bouts, but ended up each time with a bloody nose.'

Owen's fierce will to win at least had a healthy outlet as he was growing up. With just 14 years separating the five kids, they were always up to something, and Michael would often play two-on-two with his dad and his brothers even with the massive age gap of nine years between him and Andy. Michael would usually be on his dad's team, and playing against his brothers was good practice for him as he spent his early years playing against much older boys and young men, and has spent his entire career up against considerably bigger defenders.

Michael began playing competitive football with Mold Alexander Under-10s when he was still only seven. And with competitive football came his first pair of boots. 'They were "Keegan Kids" boots and cost about a tenner. I was thrilled and couldn't wait to put them on. After that first game in the park I was completely hooked and didn't want to do or think about anything except football.'

While at Mold he had his first taste of regional football as he was selected to play for Hawarden Pathfinders every couple of months. His performances at club and regional level made quite an impression on his dad. 'He'd play with boys who were a lot older than him. He'd put the ball in the corner of the net, side-footing it in, and I thought, "Blooming 'eck, what have we got here?" He wasn't chasing the ball all over the place. He'd choose a spot. He'd pass the ball into the net from an early age. He wouldn't just take a swing and hope for the best.'

He was first chosen to represent Deeside Schools, an under-11s county side, at the age of eight. In doing so he became the youngest boy ever to be picked for his county, beating a record previously held by Wales midfielder Gary Speed.

Deeside manager Bryn fondly remembers his schoolboy superstar. 'He's an all-round player but it's his pace which makes him so incredible. There wasn't a lot I had to teach Michael – he was a natural.'

Owen was made captain in his second season. He played every match and bagged 50-odd goals from just 30-something games. But he still saved the best for last as, aged 11, in his third and final season for Deeside Schools, he beat Ian Rush's record for goals in a season with 92.

Rush was a hero on Merseyside and throughout Wales, but, as Owen was growing up, it was another striker he looked to emulate. Gary Lineker was Everton's leading striker in 1985-86 and he was one of England's many heroes at the 1990 World Cup. 'My first hero was Gary Lineker,' Owen revealed. 'My first real memories of the World Cup are from 1990. I was only nine or ten at the time, and I remember running home from school every day to watch the games from Italy. Lineker, of course, scored some great goals for England in the World Cup, and it was always my ambition to follow him into the team one day. But it wasn't just the England games that fascinated me – it was everything about the atmosphere of the World Cup that totally enthralled me.'

Owen was soon on the road to the England team himself, as he attended a trial for the Football Association's School of Excellence at Lilleshall. His chance to impress came at Chester City's Deva Stadium on a cold and blustery evening, where the youngsters played in four twenty-minute matches. The conditions were so poor it would have been difficult to tell the difference between a Ronaldinho and a Martin Keown, but either Owen did enough or his reputation preceded him, and he was selected for the FA's Academy.

The dream of playing professionally was growing ever more tangible: recent graduates in the years before Owen arrived included Ian Walker, Sol Campbell, Andy Cole and Nick Barmby. Wes Brown, Michael Ball and Steve Haslam were all in Owen's year.

Owen impressed everybody with his performances on the pitch and he scored on his England Under-15s debut, a trick he would later repeat for the Under-16s and Liverpool. The goals were coming in copious quantities and most of them were of high quality, but one stood head and shoulders above the rest of his schoolboy strikes.

Playing against Scotland in Newcastle on 28 April 1995, Owen scored the goal he still regards as his finest ever. England opened the scoring but the visitors hit back, and from the restart Owen accelerated past a couple of opposition players before cutting inside a third. Approaching the penalty area, he beat one centre-back with a drop of the shoulder and sidestepped the challenge of the other centre-half before smashing the ball into the far top corner from the edge of the six-yard box. A truly memorable goal to grace the magnificent St James' Park.

Owen remembers it well. 'They'd just equalised and, from the kick-off, Kenny Lunt pushed the ball to me. I was just about to tap it back to him when he suddenly shouted at me to run. I looked up and half of the Scottish lads were still celebrating on the right-hand side of the pitch, so there were only about five to beat. I started running, went past the lot and whacked the ball into the top corner.

'Obviously it's not the most important goal I've ever scored, but certainly the best – better than the Argentina goal. I've got a video of it, and I watched it all the time for about three years until I broke into the Liverpool team.'

As well as games for his country, Owen also played the occasional game for the youth team at Liverpool, where he was on Centre of Excellence forms. And, during the 1995–6 season, Owen played for the Reds in their successful FA Youth Cup campaign. Although it was an Under-18s competition, the England Under-16s goalscorer's burgeoning talent had caught the attention of the Liverpool coaches and they got him released from Lilleshall for their tilt at glory.

In a team that included David Thompson and Jamie Carragher, Owen's first game was in the fourth round against Sheffield United and he scored two goals in a 3–2 win. After such a promising display it was of little surprise when the England lad was requested for the fifth-round tie with Manchester United at Anfield. It was another 3–2 victory but this time the young striker went one better and bagged a hat-trick.

Just as Robbie Fowler had been dubbed the new Ian Rush when he made the breakthrough at Anfield, Owen, because of his goals for the youth team, was likened to Fowler, the man the Kop referred to as 'God'. Ignoring the new attention, the youngster maintained his prolific form to ensure it wasn't too harsh a comparison.

After five goals in his first two Youth Cup games, Owen's place in the starting line-up was assured and he further justified his selection in the semi-final with three goals over two legs against Crystal Palace. Owen missed the first leg of the final against West Ham because he was on international duty, but his teammates managed without him and won 2–0 at Upton Park. Owen returned for the game at Anfield, but Liverpool got off to the worst possible start as Frank Lampard halved the aggregate deficit in the first minute, blasting home from outside the area as he so often does now. Owen was not to be denied his first piece of silverware, though, and equalised five minutes before the break. He was first to react when Hammers' keeper Neil Finn beat out a shot from Stuart Quinn and the England youngster nodded the ball home, in front of 20,000 people.

Facing Rio Ferdinand for the first time in his career, Owen found time to return the favour to his strike partner and, in the fifty-fourth minute, his shot came off the post and Quinn was perfectly positioned to score. The match ended 2–1 on the night and 4–1 on aggregate to give Liverpool the FA Youth Cup for the first time in their history.

'I was proud to be part of the first Liverpool team to win the Youth Cup,' he said. 'It is the biggest tournament for young players and you certainly got a great feeling before the games and in the games.'

The youth team manager, Steve Heighway, was delighted with his young striker. 'Owen has scored fantastic goals because his finishing is so clinical,' he said. 'He's single-minded and a bit of a free spirit. How far he goes is up to him.'

As his domestic season drew to a close, Owen went to France for the European Under-18s Championship. England got their tournament off to a slow start with two draws, first 0–0 against Spain and then 1–1 with Italy as Owen revealed the bristling character beneath his innocent exterior.

Gennaro Gattuso, who would become of the world's finest midfielders at AC Milan, opened the scoring for the Italians after fifty-five minutes, but the lead lasted just five minutes as Coventry's Andrew Ducros levelled the scores. The match ended in controversy, though, as Owen was lucky to stay on the pitch after appearing to strike Claudio Mastrapasqua, who had been holding him back. This was just seconds after sweeper Marco Pecorari had been sent off for a trip on Owen and the Liverpool striker was thankful the referee didn't see him lash out.

A 1–0 win over Ireland saw England qualify for the third-place play-off, where they beat Belgium 3–2, Owen scoring the winning goal in extra time.

Owen received his GCSE results that summer and, although he hadn't applied himself to his schoolwork with the same dedication and devotion as he showed on the football pitch, he still managed to pass all 10 with C and D grades. 'You hear a lot of people saying how important school qualifications are, but I didn't seem to see the sense in that,' he said. 'If I didn't make it as a professional footballer then I would want to do something in football.'

Meanwhile, Owen had yet to sign forms with Liverpool and many other clubs were interested in signing him. He met with Alex Ferguson at Manchester United, George Graham at Arsenal and Glenn Hoddle at Chelsea, and had trials at plenty of other clubs: Everton, Wrexham, Chester, Oldham, Norwich and Manchester City. But Liverpool made him feel most at home and Steve Heighway in particular made an excellent impression on the Owens with his honest, straight-talking approach, so Owen rewarded the Reds' hospitality by joining the Anfield playing staff.

He signed YTS (Youth Training Scheme) forms with Liverpool on a weekly wage of £42.50, and his return to North Wales helped to kick-start a romance with the 'girl next door', Louise Bonsall. The Bonsalls lived a stone's throw from the Owens, and Louise and Michael had been at school together and had known each other for a long time. But it was only when the 16-year-old Owen returned from Lilleshall that things progressed.

When Owen spotted Louise in a local pub, he sent a friend over to find out if she was still interested – and the rest is history.

2

It didn't take long for Michael Owen to force himself into the Liverpool team, and from there he was fast-tracked into the England team as his pace and prolific goalscoring drew him many admirers. Even before he had made his Liverpool debut, Owen was the subject of a transfer bid. When the Reds signed Patrik Berger from Borussia Dortmund, the German club made enquiries as to Owen's availability but were swiftly rebuffed. 'I was amazed they'd heard of him,' Anfield chief executive Peter Robinson recalled.

Still only 16 years old, Owen spent much of the early part of the 1996-97 season splitting his time between Liverpool's youth team and the England Under-18s. With his development continuing unabated, the Reds were very keen to have their prodigy signed to professional forms as soon as possible, so, on 18 December 1996, four days after his 17th birthday, Owen put pen to paper on a three-year deal.

At a stroke of his pen, Liverpool's new signing went from £42.50 to £400-a-week and received a £5,000 signing bonus. He treated himself to a new car, a Rover Coupé, and, ever the generous lad, took his parents and his little sister on holiday to Spain. But the most exciting thing for the youngster was his promotion to training with the first team and his new squad number: 18.

Owen was included in a Premiership squad for the first time, away to Sunderland on 13 April 1997 and made the bench, but wasn't required as Liverpool won 2–1. On 6 May 1997, Owen made his Premiership debut, and marked the occasion with his first senior goal for Liverpool. With only 10 reserve appearances to his name, he was brought on to try to save a game that was drifting away from the Reds and taking their hopes of a first Premiership title with it. Liverpool needed two wins from their last two games to have any hope of catching Manchester United, and they were trailing to Jason Euell's header at the break. Owen had just been told to warm up when Wimbledon scored again, through Dean Holdsworth. Desperate for the three points, Evans took Patrik Berger off after 59 minutes and put his teenage striker upfront with Collymore.

In the 74th minute, Owen ran onto a Stig Inge Bjornebye through-ball and applied a cool finish. Unfortunately, Liverpool couldn't muster any more magic like that and their title drought continued.

Owen made his full debut on the last day of the season, alongside Collymore in a 1–1 draw at Sheffield Wednesday. Collymore was substituted at half-time, leaving the 17-year-old Owen upfront with the veteran John Barnes, and it proved to be Collymore's last appearance for Liverpool.

Having surrendered the league in the previous match, Liverpool had now given away the Champions League place that had been theirs for the taking. But Owen was delighted to have made his first appearances for the Reds, and overjoyed at claiming his first Premiership goal, but

before he could enjoy a summer holiday the striker joined up with his young England teammates at the World Youth Under-20s Championship in Malaysia.

He scored in each of the group games in Johor Bahru as the young Lions sailed through Group F with maximum points. In the last 16 they faced Argentina, who, inspired by Juan Roman Riquelme and Pablo Aimar, took a 2–0 lead into the break. Despite Jamie Carragher's goal early in the second half, England couldn't find an equaliser and Argentina maintained their impressive World Youth Championship form, going on to win the cup for a third time.

Before the new season started, the Liverpool manager replaced Stan Collymore with Karlheinz Riedle from Borussia Dortmund. Owen couldn't expect to be starting ahead of Fowler or Riedle, but his chances took on a much brighter complexion when Fowler picked up an ankle injury before the opening day, giving the youngster another opportunity to impress.

Facing Wimbledon again, Owen made it two from two at Selhurst Park, as he scored a 71st-minute penalty in a game that finished 1–1. He got his second of the season two weeks later as he hit a 52nd-minute goal against Blackburn at Ewood Park, in another 1–1 draw. But the young striker's fiery streak was revealed for the first time in his professional career in early September as Owen was sent off while captaining England Under-18s at Rotherham. There were only 20 minutes on the clock when Owen lost his rag. The Liverpool lad had been kicked all over the pitch from the start and, when he retaliated with a head butt to yet another foul from the Yugoslavian defenders, he was rightly shown the red card.

A week later Owen scored six minutes into his European

debut against Glasgow Celtic, with many of his Scottish relatives watching the game at Celtic Park. Owen's form impressed his family and also the manager – so much so that Evans decided to drop Riedle when Fowler returned from injury and the youngster kept his place in the team.

His first professional goal at Anfield came against Tottenham, scoring in the 88th minute of a 4–0 romp. There was more good news the following week as he joined the full England squad for training at Bisham Abbey. Unavailable to play due to the ban he picked up for his sending off against Yugoslavia Under-18s, Owen was called up by England manager Glenn Hoddle to rub shoulders with his heroes ahead of their game against Cameroon.

The goals kept coming for Liverpool's bright new talent and, although he had been forced to wait for his first professional strike at Anfield, Owen soon had plenty more to go with it as he hit a hat-trick in the next match, a League Cup tie against Grimsby Town.

'To wrap my hat-trick up with my first goal at the Kop end was magnificent. Now I hope I can score a few more hat-tricks,' he said. 'Glenn Hoddle's encouraged me to enjoy the experience of training with the England squad and hopefully I can now push my way into the team. I think I could do a job for him.'

His first game with the England Under-21s was in the second leg of a crucial European Championship play-off against Greece. The Young Lions had lost the away leg 2–0 and, although they won the return 4–2, they were out on the away-goals rule. It was a good night for Owen on a personal level, though, as he once again scored on a debut with his 60th-minute strike. It proved to be his one and

only Under-21s cap but it helped the Liverpool forward to complete his record of playing for England at each of the representative age groups.

By the time he turned 18, Own had scored nine times for Liverpool. The games were coming thick and fast for Owen and he caught the eye of a Kop legend when he scored again to beat Newcastle at Anfield. Jason McAteer released Owen in the inside-left channel, and the youngster took a couple of strides forward before stroking the ball past the advancing Shaka Hislop and into the top corner of the goal. The game finished 1–0, and despite the result, Newcastle boss Kenny Dalglish couldn't fail to be impressed by the new Prince of the Kop. 'Owen had no right to finish like that,' he said.

With six wins and a draw in their last seven league games, the three points put Liverpool level with Blackburn in second place, five points behind Manchester United. Always keen to improve, Owen had been spongelike since his Premiership debut, soaking up tips and tricks to maximise his ability.

'I'm always learning,' he said. 'I watch Robbie and Karlheinz and I think I've definitely improved. They recognise I'm a young lad and they help me and make me feel comfortable. I'm playing with and against world-class players every week so there has to be improvement.'

Owen's ability brought a call-up to the full England squad. He was playing golf when he heard the news from Liverpool coach Doug Livermore.

'I knew the squad was being announced and, although you are not supposed to use mobiles out on the course, I switched mine on for a short while. When Doug rang, it was a truly amazing feeling for me. Then the phone went another 20 times in the next ten minutes, so I had to switch it off.'

With the World Cup just four months away, Owen was included in the 24-man squad for a game against Chile. He celebrated his call-up with a brace against Southampton in a 3–2 loss at home. The young striker was absolutely superb that day, but his teammates weren't up to scratch and the defeat effectively ended Liverpool's title aspirations.

With only 33 appearances for Liverpool, Owen was light on experience and, at 18 years and 59 days, he became the youngest England international of the 20th century, breaking Duncan Edwards's record, which had stood since 1955, by 124 days. Since he had played at Wembley twice before – against Brazil and Germany in his schoolboy days, and scored on each occasion – the omens were good. Owen also scored on his debut at Under-15, -16, -18, -20 and -21 levels for England, but sadly he couldn't repeat the trick against Chile as the South Americans won 2–0.

The debutant was realistic in defeat. 'It wasn't a good team performance,' Owen said, 'but I feel I did all right.'

Hoddle accentuated the positive. 'I thought Owen acquitted himself very well. He's only 18, but he's shown he can get off markers in the last third of the pitch. He performed as well as anybody against a very organised Chilean side, who were tough defensively.'

As Owen's fortunes continued to rise, Liverpool's were taking a downturn: the Reds were knocked out of the League Cup by Middlesbrough and then drew with Everton as Fowler's damaged knee ligaments put him out of action for the rest of the season and the ensuing World Cup.

Losing their leading scorer as results were going against them wasn't great news for Liverpool, but it meant that Owen was all but assured of a place in the team for the rest of the season, and it took another striker out of the running for the England squad.

The admirers were queuing up to push Owen's cause for a World Cup place, including his boyhood hero Gary Lineker.

'Owen is an awesome talent,' the former England striker said. 'Even at my peak, I never had the trickery or pace he's got. Glenn Hoddle says he probably won't get as many goals as I did because I was a natural scorer and there's far more to Owen's game than just that. Owen's the sort of player who can come on for the last 20 minutes and change the game, and that could be mighty useful in the World Cup.'

April started brightly for Owen, as he was announced as the Professional Footballers' Association (PFA) Young Player of the Year. His 19 goals so far in the season, 14 of which came in the Premiership, and the promising start to his England career had seen him come out on top of the vote by his peers, beating Southampton's Kevin Davies and West Ham's Rio Ferdinand into second and third place respectively.

But Owen was making headlines for all the wrong reasons five days later as he was shown a red card at Old Trafford. He'd opened the scoring after 36 minutes, but was running around like a madman, and even clattered into Peter Schmeichel – which certainly isn't sensible when you're five foot eight and less than 11 stone. Owen unsurprisingly came off second best in the collision with the Great Dane, but he still hadn't learned his lesson and caught Ronny Johnsen very late and was justifiably sent off.

Poor Johnsen was taken to hospital and Manchester United took advantage of their numerical superiority to rescue a draw, 1–1.

Owen kept scoring for Liverpool as he took his total to

21 for the season against Coventry. He earned his third England cap as a late substitute against Portugal, and it was his electrifying performance against a tiring defence that truly showed he was ready for international football. England were leading 3–0 against arguably the best team not to qualify for the World Cup, when Owen replaced Sheringham with 13 minutes left. In that short time he twice went close to claiming his first England goal, and even had what looked like a legitimate penalty appeal turned down.

Having started the season with the ambition of starting a dozen Liverpool games, Owen had played 44 times for the Reds, starting 41 matches and scoring 23 goals. In the Premiership he had scored 18 from his 36 games, to share the Golden Boot with Dion Dublin and Blackburn's Chris Sutton. He was named PFA Young Player of the Year and Carling Premiership Player of the Year. He forced his way through the England Under-21s and into the full team despite being just 18 years old, and he was part of the squad travelling to Morocco for England's World Cup warm-up matches.

Owen's future looked bright, and Liverpool's all-time leading goalscorer was already worried about his records. 'When Robbie Fowler first came into the Liverpool team I said he was capable of smashing all my scoring records,' Ian Rush said. 'That still applies because he's only 22, but now you can add Michael's name to the list because he's four years younger. Liverpool are very fortunate to have two strikers so young and gifted. It must be frightening for the rest of the Premiership because the best is yet to come from the pair of them.'

At the World Cup in France, Michael Owen would show just what he was capable of.

3

Michael Owen went into the 1998 World Cup as an enthusiastic and incredibly talented 18-year-old, but he left the tournament as a national hero and a household name across the footballing world. His goal against Argentina took him from anonymity to global acclaim and by the time he stepped off the plane back in England, his life had been changed for ever.

He wasn't even in the starting line-up for England's first game in France but by the knockout stage he was one of the key players in the side. At just 18 years and 164 days old, Owen had become England's youngest goalscorer in a warm-up match against Morocco – a record later beaten by Wayne Rooney.

On the eve of the tournament, Hoddle offered his appraisal of Owen's attributes, presciently comparing him to the best player in the world at the time in his ability to run with the ball. 'Ronaldo likes to collect the ball and turn to run at defenders,' Hoddle said. 'You can see Owen do that because there are a lot of strings to his bow. He brings us a different dimension. He can start and influence the game. But if he comes on via the bench he can give us something different to anything we've got in the squad.

'At this moment he is being educated in international football and he will develop through this World Cup. He has to develop better awareness at this level and learn how to get off the hook if he is being tightly marked. He has two major assets – genuine pace with the ball and without it, but he also has good movement way beyond his age. Pace with good movement is rare.'

England got off to a comfortable 2–0 win against Tunisia, with Shearer and Sheringham up front. Owen came on for six minutes but was on the bench again for the next match against Romania in Toulouse. This time, with England trailing 1–0, he was sent on with 17 minutes remaining in a bid to save the match. It worked; 10 minutes later, Owen was on hand to bury Shearer's cutback. He came close again when he hit the post from 25 yards in injury time, but it was not his day to be the hero. Chelsea's Dan Petrescu had put Romania 2–1 up in the 90th minute and when Owen's long-range effort came back off the woodwork, English hopes of saving the game died.

Hoddle brought in Owen and David Beckham in place of Sheringham and David Batty for the last group game against Colombia, with the country's best 11 players together for the first time, the fans were rewarded with England's finest performance of the tournament. They completely outplayed Colombia from start to finish and won 2–0, with first-half goals from Darren Anderton and Beckham.

England finished second in the group and would face Argentina in the next round. The highly rated Albicelestes

('White and Sky Blues') were one of a handful of sides with real hopes of winning the tournament and very daunting opponents for that early stage. The striking prowess of Gabriel Batistuta, the creative genius of Juan Sebastián Verón, and Roberto Ayala's staunch defending formed the spine of the side that was looking to topple England.

But England took on Argentina in a confident mood. There were a lot more chances than were to be expected, and Owen certainly made the most of them, but first blood went to Argentina. With just five minutes on the clock, Diego Simeone tumbled over David Seaman's outstretched arms and the referee pointed to the spot. As one of the finest goalscorers in Serie A, Batistuta was expected to score, and he did just that, although Seaman managed to get his hands to the ball as it crossed the line.

Barely four minutes after going behind, England were level. Scholes sent a looping pass for Owen to run onto and as the youngster entered the box he fell under Ayala's body check. Just as Simeone had gone looking for a penalty at one end, Owen had gone looking for one at the other, running across the defender and falling under the inevitable impact. Nielsen again pointed to the spot, and Shearer drilled his penalty into the top corner. Having manufactured the equaliser with his lightning pace it was time for Owen to take centre stage and score the goal that will stay with him for the rest of his life.

There were just 16 minutes on the clock when Owen scored the third goal of the game, but, unlike the two penalties that had come before, this was a goal of beautiful magnificence that will burn brightly in the memories of all who saw it. Loitering just inside the opposition half, Owen received Beckham's pass in behind the Argentine midfield and, after controlling the ball with the outside of his right foot, he accelerated towards goal. The South American defenders were scared to tackle the youngster; Ayala and José Chamot backed off and Owen surged forward. As he approached the box he knocked the ball past Ayala and left him for dead.

Ignoring the shouts of Paul Scholes calling for a pass, he closed on the ball and clipped it goalwards from just inside the box. The ball sailed past Carlos Roa into the top left corner of the goal and the youngster wheeled away in celebration. He ran and ran and was mobbed on the halfway line by his teammates just in front of where his family were seated in the crowd.

Against two seasoned campaigners from Italy's Serie A, Owen had turned the game on its head with two runs at the opposition defence in the space of six minutes. By tormenting Lazio's Chamot and Ayala of Napoli, he had shown he could perform against some of the world's best defenders and, by doing it in the second round of the World Cup finals, he had shown he was a man for the big occasion.

But the game was far from over. In first-half injury time, Javier Zanetti levelled the scores from a cleverly worked free-kick routine, and in the 47th minute came the second memorable moment from the epic encounter. Beckham was sent off for retaliating to a foul by Simeone and England were forced to play the remainder of the game with ten men.

In the 81st minute England thought they had won the game, but Campbell's headed goal from a corner was disallowed for Shearer's challenge on the keeper. As Owen and some of his teammates mobbed Campbell in celebration, the opposition took the free kick and broke quickly. Verón surged dangerously into the England half, but Anderton came to the rescue with a vital interception and the other players recovered to relieve the pressure.

Owen had a chance to win the game in extra time, but couldn't reproduce his first-half heroics and he shot over the bar after breaking free of the defence. With neither side able to break the deadlock, the game drew inevitably to penalties.

Owen took England's fourth and sent it grazing the woodwork on its way into the net – an unstoppable effort. But Ince and Batty weren't so blessed, and England were out of the tournament.

The press knew who their scapegoat was for England's disappointment: Ten brave lions, one stupid boy, ran the *Daily Mirror* headline, as they and the other tabloids laid the blame squarely at Beckham's feet. But Owen and the rest of the players were united behind their teammate.

'All that stick David is getting is not deserved,' Owen told the *News of the World*. 'I know what he's going through because I was there myself. It's not a nice feeling. He made a mistake, but he will learn from it. Nobody in the England camp blames him.' Owen had seen how much Beckham was suffering and empathised strongly with his future captain. But the feeling throughout the rest of the footballing world was of disappointment, as the World Cup was now robbed of one of its brightest talents – Owen was heading home.

'That's the sad thing,' Hoddle said. 'He would have become even more known worldwide if we'd have continued in this tournament.'

Owen had signed a new boot deal just days before the tournament started, but with his profile soaring there was talk of how much money he could earn in the next year. Early estimates put the combined revenue from advertisements, endorsements, book deals, wages and the boot deal somewhere in eight figures, when barely 18 months before the young striker had been a YTS trainee on £42.50 a week.

Rachel Anderson, a football agent, said in *The Times*, 'For advertisers he is too good to be true – handsome, well mannered, loyal to his schoolgirl sweetheart and a brilliant player. He can easily earn £10 million this year, but should take his time and wait for the most lucrative and prestigious deals.'

His life truly had changed forever. Not even a regular at Anfield before Fowler's injury, Owen had forced his way into the England team and, barring injury, would be one of the first names on the team sheet for many years to come. Although his first World Cup outing had ended in disappointment, at the tender age of eighteen, football's newest superstar would surely have many more chances to impress on the grand stage.

4

It wasn't just the fans and the photographers who were taking more interest in English football's new star: Europe's biggest clubs had spent the second half of the summer trying to prise Owen away from Liverpool, with talk of £50 million bids. But Liverpool weren't interested in selling and Owen had decided to stay at Anfield, committed to the club that had given him his breakthrough and unwilling to move away from his tight-knit family at such a young age.

But there were changes at Liverpool that summer. Gérard Houllier came in as joint manager alongside Roy Evans. After four years in sole charge, the boot room boy had been unable to bring the club the league title they had craved so much since their last win in 1990. And, having seen the great work done at Highbury by Arsène Wenger, the men in charge of the club decided to bring in a top Continental coach. Houllier had taken Lens from the French Second Division to the top flight and even into the UEFA Cup, before winning the French title with Paris St Germain and then becoming technical director of the national side.

The Frenchman had worked in Liverpool before and even classed himself as a Reds fan after spending a year as an assistant at Alsop Comprehensive School in 1969-70, as part of his degree at Lille University.

Houllier's first task was to rid the Reds of their 'Spice Boys' image and make them a more disciplined and professional outfit. The days of players getting blind drunk every weekend were drawing to a close as England increasingly fell in line with the rest of Europe and their more health-conscious approach to sport. In came more stretching, better physical conditioning, more attention to diet and preparation and eventually an increased standard of football throughout the country.

At a friendly tournament in Ireland, Liverpool beat local side St Patrick's and then Leeds, who had knocked out Lazio, to win the Carlsberg Trophy at Lansdowne Road. Owen and Steve McManaman both scored in the 2–0 victory over the Yorkshire side, and, despite the midfielder's influential match, it was Owen who received the man-of-the-match award. The striker was obviously embarrassed to take the plaudits, not for the first time since St Etienne, and Liverpool's joint manager Evans was concerned about his protégé. 'I think it gets to him that he's being picked out from the rest of the lads all the time,' he said.

Of all the deals offered Owen's way, the most significant had to be his new five-year contract to stay at Liverpool. Worth a reputed £20,000 per week, it bound him to Liverpool into the next millennium. Owen was fully committed to Liverpool, and couldn't wait for the season to start. Having worn No. 9 throughout his early career, he had been given John Barnes's old No. 10 shirt for the new campaign and it was the same number he would dominate for England over the next decade.

With his new shirt and his new contract, Owen was desperate to prove he was no flash in the pan, and his first chance to prove that was away to Southampton on 16 August. Owen crossed for Riedle to score the first goal before he claimed the winner himself in the second half of the 2–1 victory. It was the perfect way to remind people of his footballing ability as the season got under way, and there was plenty more to come.

Owen scored a first-half hat-trick in a 4–1 win over Newcastle, after which Hoddle declared, 'He's the top striker in the country at the moment.' Then he helped his club to the top of the table in his 50th competitive appearance as they beat Coventry 2–0 at Anfield. Patrik Berger and Jamie Redknapp scored the goals, but Owen had two efforts ruled out for offside.

The England man got another goal when Liverpool travelled to Slovakia to play FC Kosice in the UEFA Cup, winning 3–0, and travelled to Old Trafford determined to make up for his aberration during his last visit. 'I was sent off and I blame myself for that,' Owen said. 'I may have cost the team two extra points, even though they did well to hang on. I now hope to put that right.'

But Owen had little opportunity to make amends during a 2–0 defeat and things weren't much better with England as they struggled through their qualifying campaign for Euro 2000. Hoddle's team followed up a 2–1 defeat in Sweden with a dour 0–0 draw against Bulgaria at Wembley. But four days later Luxembourg were a little less solid opposition and the young striker got his fourth international goal in a 3–0 win.

The goals showed signs that Shearer and Owen were developing as a partnership, though there were grave doubts about how well the two goalscorers complemented each other. 'If we work at it, we can always put it right,' Owen said. 'People said that Robbie Fowler and I couldn't play together at Liverpool, but we have a pretty decent record.

'Alan helps me all the time. Some people might let a young player go and make mistakes and then tell them afterwards what they were doing wrong. But he's tried to stop me making them in the first place.'

Owen certainly had a better chance of scoring when he was actually playing matches, and that wasn't the case back with Liverpool, as Houllier and Evans decided to rest the young striker for the UEFA Cup tie with Valencia. He was missed in a 0–0 draw with the Spaniards but he came back refreshed and scored four goals in his next game.

Nottingham Forest were the unfortunate opponents who had to contend with a revitalised Owen, and he opened the scoring at Anfield after ten minutes as the Reds went on to win 5–1. 'Whether it was right to leave me out is debatable,' he said. 'A lot of people have said what they think about it, and the managers decided to give me a rest. On this evidence it looks as if it's paid off. But I'm young and I want to play in every match.'

Liverpool squeezed past Valencia on the away-goals rule after drawing 2–2 in Spain, but the busy year caught up with Owen as he limped out of the League Cup defeat at home to Tottenham. He scored after 81 minutes but then pulled his hamstring and faced a spell on the sidelines for the first time since his breakthrough at Selhurst Park 18 months before.

While Owen was out, Evans left Liverpool, after the Reds had slipped to 12th in the Premiership, leaving Houllier in sole command. Meanwhile, England beat the Czech Republic 2–0.

Owen's return coincided with Houllier's first game in sole charge, a 4–2 win over Aston Villa. It was the first defeat Villa had suffered all season and, coming at home in their 13th game, it showed that Liverpool were turning their massive potential into results at last. And there was a spirit of togetherness in the Liverpool camp.

The Owen-Fowler partnership was bearing fruit now, though. In the 39 games the pair had featured in together, they had contributed 32 goals. Fowler had 18 of those and Owen 14, but it showed that a partnership that many thought wouldn't work out was proving to be quite devastating.

On the eve of his 19th birthday, Owen was named the BBC Sports Personality of the Year. It was a fantastic present, and led Owen to look retrospectively at all he had achieved in the past 12 months. 'My life changed after that goal. Even now it's all people want to talk about when I meet them for the first time. It's something that will be with me forever. Even if it's the only thing I do in my career, it's not a bad thing to be remembered for, is it?'

'The strange thing is, that while I was being compared with Ronaldo and Pele in the summer, a few months later I was being told I wasn't worth a place in the England side after the friendly against Bulgaria at Wembley. That has taught me how important it is not to get carried away by all the praise and glory.'

His FA Cup dream was soon ended as the Reds lost to Manchester United at Old Trafford in the fourth round. Owen did maintain his 100 per cent record in the competition with the opener after three minutes, but the Red Devils hit back to win 2–1.

Owen responded in fine form and scored in the 7–1 thrashing of Southampton, and a win over Middlesbrough. But Liverpool's form was incredibly inconsistent as they suffered away defeats to Coventry and Charlton.

On 2 February 1999, Glenn Hoddle was sacked as England manager. With only eight days before England's next match, there wasn't enough time for the FA to secure a full-time replacement, so Howard Wilkinson took temporary charge for the match against World Cup holders France. Owen started alongside Shearer but neither of them could find a way through the experienced defence as the visitors kept a clean sheet and England lost 2–0. The press at Wembley took it as a sign that Wilkinson wasn't up to the job permanently, and increased their vociferous calls for Kevin Keegan to take control. The former European Footballer of the Year eventually bowed to public opinion and took the job on a part-time basis, while continuing in his role as manager of Fulham.

Keegan initially took the reins for just four games – the World Cup qualifiers against Poland, Hungary, Sweden and Bulgaria – but in May he decided to leave Fulham and assume full-time control of the national team. Owen didn't play under the new manager until September, due to injury, and whether or not that lack of game time had any effect on the relationship between the pair is uncertain, but it is clear that Keegan had very little confidence in the diminutive striker and Owen didn't enjoy his time under the passionate but somewhat unpredictable manager.

All the recurring hamstring problems that the Boy Wonder had over the next three years can be traced back to an insufficient recovery following the injury Owen sustained against Leeds in April 1999. Somewhat prophetically, his manager spoke at the time of his intention to avoid future complications. 'The scan has revealed damage to the hamstring and the tendon,' Houllier said. 'The doctors say it is an injury he has had before and I am very aware that I do not want it to become a chronic problem for him during his career.'

Owen's recuperation was a source of dispute between Houllier and the club physio, Mark Leather, and Leather eventually left the club halfway through pre-season. Before he departed, he had been at odds with the manager regarding the amount, or lack thereof, of strength work Owen was doing on his injured leg. Without a physio to consult, Owen's convalescence faltered and when the new season started the fleet-footed forward had insufficient strength in his leg to sprint as he had previously, and the inevitable breakdowns followed.

At the tail end of the 1998-99 season, Owen missed Liverpool's last seven league matches, as well as three England games. Manchester United won the league, finishing one point ahead of Arsenal, and Liverpool finished 25 points behind the Champions, in seventh. The Reds' 'transitional' season was highlighted by the fact that they would not be in Europe the following season, after finishing below West Ham and Aston Villa, only two points ahead of Derby County.

Despite missing almost 20 per cent of the league season, Owen still finished as the Premiership top scorer and shared the Golden Boot with Jimmy Floyd Hasselbaink and Dwight Yorke, who had also scored 18 league goals. Owen could look back on a successful year in front of goal. A Golden Boot winner after playing in only 30 games, he had followed up his incredible World Cup debut with 23 goals from 40 appearances in all competitions.

After attracting so much attention the previous summer, Owen had cemented his position as England's most dangerous forward with another bagful of goals, and if Liverpool were to keep his services they would need to improve – fast.

5

Michael Owen had had a tough year with injuries, but as it drew to a close things were looking up, and he could begin to look forward to the European Championship.

'Everything seems to be slipping into place now: my fitness, strength, stamina. I'm pleased with my own progress.'

In the summer Owen had visited Dr Hans Müller-Wohlfahrt, a German hamstring-injury specialist, for further tests and treatment but had failed to make it back for the start of the season. Houllier had been very busy in the transfer market, recruiting the best part of a whole new team. In came Sander Westerveld, Sami Hyypia, Stéphane Henchoz, Didi Hamann, Emile Heskey, Titi Camara, Rigobert Song, Erik Meijer and Vladimír Smicer; gone were Steve McManaman, Paul Ince, Oyvind Leonhardsen, David James, Karlheinz Riedle, Rob Jones, Jean-Michel Ferri, Tony Warner and Bjørn Tore Kvarme.

So when Owen returned to action, it was in a very different first XI from those of his last appearance. Of the new players, the one man whom Owen bonded with most quickly was Hamann. The German midfielder shared

Owen's twin loves away from football, horses and golf, and, from the moment the former Newcastle player walked into the training ground with the *Racing Post* under his arm, a close friendship was formed.

Owen was recruited by the team behind England's bid for the 2006 World Cup. The Liverpool attacker handed the proposal to the FIFA president Sepp Blatter, and took to the ambassadorial role with aplomb. He also turned his hand to acting, playing himself in a BBC children's television show called *Hero to Zero*. 'I used to love watching programmes like that when I was a kid. It'll now be great to be part of one,' he said.

Nearing full fitness, he was selected for the England squad to face Luxembourg and Poland, and was then named in the Liverpool squad to face Arsenal. Four and a half months after tearing his hamstring against Leeds, Owen was overjoyed to return to action at Anfield. But with only two brief appearances in the reserves since his injury, he was coming back a little underprepared in his manager's eyes. 'It's a bit too soon for Michael, and he knows that,' Houllier told the press. 'But at the same time, for himself and for the club and for his country, we need him, and we'll maybe need to rush his comeback a bit sooner than we would want.'

Owen came on late in a 2–0 win over the Gunners, and, although he wasn't among the goalscorers, he was delighted to be back playing for his club, and he followed that up with a rapid return to action for his country. With only one cap since the match in Luxembourg 11 months previously, and only a handful of Premiership minutes since May, Owen was understandably left on the bench, but that didn't stop him grabbing his first senior goal at Wembley.

Desperate for three points after their woeful start to the qualifying campaign, England were 5–0 up at half-time. Owen replaced Beckham after 64 minutes and put the cherry on the top of a sweet victory, curling home right-footed from outside the area in the last minute.

'It was a great feeling to score,' he said. 'I haven't scored a goal for about five or six months so it was a great feeling to get back on the pitch, especially playing in an international at Wembley. I've scored for the junior teams here before but never for the senior side at Wembley.'

Keegan decided to use Owen as a substitute again for the crunch tie against Poland, but neither he nor any of his teammates could find a way through the stubborn Polish defence, and the game finished 0–0. The result left England level on points with the Poles, but ahead by virtue of the head-to-head results between the countries. Having played their last game, England needed Sweden to beat Poland the following month to guarantee a second-place finish in Group 5 and a place in the play-offs.

Liverpool's dismal Premiership form was then highlighted as they lost 3–2 to Manchester United and then lost the Merseyside derby 1–0 to Everton at Anfield. It was a fractious game, blighted by three red cards, and Owen was very lucky that the ref didn't make it four after he committed a hideous two-footed challenge on David Weir.

There was better news on the international front, where a 2–0 win for the Swedes over Poland had salvaged England's hopes of qualifying for Euro 2000 in Holland and Belgium. The players watched the game together the day before their match against Belgium and they celebrated the next day by beating their possible tournament hosts 2–1.

England were struggling along at 1–1 before Owen came on for the final half an hour and turned the game on its head. It was undisputedly his top performance in an England shirt since his injury. He tormented the visitors' defence at the Stadium of Light for 30 minutes and his manager was very impressed. 'When I put Michael on I thought, "Yeah, that's the player I remember against Argentina in the World Cup",' Keegan said. 'He gave us another dimension.'

The play-off draw paired England with Scotland, the 'Auld Enemy', but as the first leg drew near there were doubts again over Owen's fitness. He had limped out of a match at The Dell with another hamstring pull, this time the left, and it was clear his problems had not gone away. Owen was determined to start against Scotland and remained bullish when asked about his injuries.

'We sort of diagnosed my hamstrings were doing a lot of work to keep my body upright and straight and the muscles around my pelvis weren't working properly,' he explained. 'So when the hamstrings were asked to run they were already tired from doing overtime. I spend half an hour before and after training stretching and strengthening these muscles and that's an ongoing process I'll do for the rest of my career.'

Owen got his first start under Keegan, and England won 2–0 at Hampden Park, thanks to a first-half brace from Paul Scholes. Having gained the upper hand in the Battle of Britain, England were expected to secure their qualification with a routine win at Wembley and let the Euro 2000 party start. But Scotland had other ideas.

Don Hutchison scored the only goal after 39 minutes, in a game that Scotland dominated. England were through, but the critics were not happy. Owen was slated in the press – declared to be rubbish in the air and have no left foot.

So he was thrilled to make a goalscoring return for Liverpool in his next match. 'It was a nice way to silence the critics,' Owen said, after grabbing the opener in a 2–0 win over Sunderland at the Stadium of Light. 'I woke up on the morning of this game finding out I wasn't so popular. At least I can say I'm popular again with the Liverpool fans.'

It was a fourth win in a row for the Reds, who were now unbeaten in seven matches, and it finally looked like Houllier's team were getting their act together. But with typically consistent inconsistency they followed up this first away win since September by losing 1–0 at West Ham. It was an especially frustrating day for Owen, who was booked for diving and had a 'goal' disallowed before being substituted, but at least he knew that, if things continued to infuriate him at club level, he had plenty of options elsewhere.

Europe's biggest spenders in 1999 were Lazio, managed by Sven-Göran Eriksson, who were linked with a £35 million move for Owen. The coach added to the speculation with his words of admiration. 'Owen is perhaps the most outstanding young player in Europe,' he said. 'He could not have a better school than Liverpool to learn the game, but if he wants to make the most of his ability he must come to Italy.'

Liverpool enjoyed a good December as they won four

and drew one of their five matches. Saint Michael of Merseyside had a fine end to the year as well, scoring four goals in the last three games, including two at St James' Park, as he found the net on 26 December for the third successive year.

Unfortunately, he was far less productive in January due to a fresh hamstring problem. It kept him out of a 1–0 defeat against Tottenham and the FA Cup fourth round exit at the hands of Blackburn, who were then outside of the Premiership. And, although Owen returned to action in a 3–2 win at Watford, he hobbled off after less than half an hour of the following match against Middlesbrough.

Liverpool were struggling without him, and it was hoped he would soon return to action following another trip to Dr Müller-Wohlfahrt in Munich. But the youngster was justifiably concerned by yet another setback. 'Obviously I'm worried because I've suffered five hamstring injuries,' Owen told the *Independent*. 'But they've not all been in the same area. I've learned now that if you play on when you feel a twinge it can quickly become a pull or a tear and I don't want what happened at Leeds last season to happen to me again.'

Owen returned to action in a 1–1 draw with Manchester United that left Liverpool 10 points behind the Red Devils, looking at another trophyless campaign. But, with 12 league games left, the Reds were still in with a good chance of a top-three finish and a place in the Champions League the following season. Two more draws, at home to Sunderland and Aston Villa, undermined those hopes but Owen then helped get Liverpool back to winning ways with the first goal in a 2–0 win away at Derby.

It was 18 March and it was his first goal of 2000, as his fitness and finishing had both been affected by some sort of millennium bug, but he quickly made it four goals in three games as Liverpool won five on the bounce to go second in the table. They beat Newcastle 2–1 at home without Owen, before he returned to make a fool out of the Coventry defence on 1 April, grabbing a first-half brace in a 3–0 win at Highfield Road.

Back to full fitness, Owen had formed a promising partnership with Emile Heskey, signed by Houllier from Leicester City in March for £11 million. The pair had previously played together in junior sides for England, and Liverpool were milking the rewards of their understanding. 'Our partnership is blossoming, and I believe we complement each other perfectly,' Owen said.

It proved the right combination a week later against Tottenham Hotspur at home, as Owen scored the winner in a 2–1 victory. It was his first goal at Anfield since Boxing Day, and it gave Liverpool a fourth win in a row. Afterwards Owen would talk only of Europe. 'I want to play amongst the elite, and that means the Champions League,' he said at the post-match press conference. 'Playing in the Champions League is something I really want. We've sat and watched Manchester United in their big games and it's made us envious. It's the same for all the Liverpool players. You watch all these top teams and you try to compare yourself to all these players.'

The run-in proved too tough for Houllier's boys, however, as they suffered a barren spell in front of goal. They failed to score in their last five games and ended up fourth in the table.

The Reds had been in with a chance of third until the final day but finished a miserable 24 points behind Manchester United, who retained their title in convincing style, 18 points ahead of their nearest rivals Arsenal, and it was clear that Liverpool would need to improve drastically if they wanted a first Championship since 1990. Houllier's side had also struggled in the cups: out of the FA Cup in the fourth round and the League Cup in the third round.

But despite his injury-hit season, the young striker still managed to score 12 goals in his 30 appearances, 11 in the League and one in the League Cup. Before he could add to his Liverpool tally, though, Owen had to contend with the Continent's finest as he travelled to the European Championship in Belgium and Holland.

6

Michael Owen headed to Euro 2000 fit and raring to go. Having barely featured in England's qualifying campaign, he was determined to make the most of his opportunities at the tournament in Holland and Belgium. But, unfortunately for him, the Three Lions were well below par, and Owen had a miserable time as his relationship with Keegan went from bad to worse.

He was most people's choice for man of the match, at least for the home side, in a warm-up match against Brazil at Wembley. He scored the first goal – an absolute gem – after 38 minutes, and throughout the game he displayed the abundant pace, energy and goalscoring instinct of his pre-injury days. But Brazil retained possession with all the effortless grace that is expected from the serial World Cup winners and claimed an equaliser in first-half stoppage time after a mistake by David Seaman.

Keegan was happy with his strike partnership. 'Michael and Alan were very lively upfront when they got the service,' the manager said. 'I saw a lot of good things with them. As regards the first Euro 2000 match, neither of them did themselves any harm.'

Yet the manager continued to dwell on those aspects missing from Owen's game. 'He is still a young player who has got a lot to learn. If I had to nit-pick, he should hold the ball up more.'

After his fine performance against Brazil, no one thought anything of Owen's absence in the following friendly against the Ukraine. It was natural for the coach to try out all of his alternatives ahead of a big tournament, and it was vital that every player should have a chance to stay match-fit. But, when Owen was then left out of the starting XI for the game against Malta, it seemed that Keegan hadn't yet made up his mind as to who would partner Shearer upfront.

'I hope I can still persuade the manager and I think I'm a big occasion player' he said bullishly. 'I'm certainly not scared about going into any game at international level against the best players in the world. I can then show what kind of a player I am. It comes naturally to me. I don't fear anyone when I go onto the pitch and, if I'm picked against Portugal in that first game, I would have no fears.'

When the day arrived, Owen was selected to start alongside Shearer and England got off to a flying start against the much-fancied Portuguese. Scholes grabbed the first after three minutes, and McManaman got the second a quarter of an hour later. But naively Keegan's team continued to attack, and Portugal caught them out with two well-taken goals from Joao Pinto and Luis Figo.

Owen had been guilty of losing the ball far too much during the opening 45 minutes, and Keegan decided to replace him with Heskey at the break. The confidence that Owen had built up with his goal in the game against Brazil had been slowly eroded, and now the manager had ripped away any remaining self-assurance with that substitution.

'When you first get brought off and replaced in a major tournament you ask yourself questions,' Owen later told the *Independent on Sunday*. 'I've been through the game thousands of times in my head, thinking about what I did well and what I didn't do well. One thing I thought is that I was the last person to touch the ball before Figo scored. But at half-time he [Keegan] told me, "You haven't done anything wrong. You're a big part of this team in this tournament. I just wanted to change the tactics and have a different option upfront. I want a different type of player. I think we need to get hold of the ball more."'

Keegan tried to heal the rift the following day by telling Owen he would start in the next game, against Germany. 'He's only young,' the manager said of Owen. 'His day will come, on Saturday.' But the youngster believed that was only because the substitution hadn't proved any more successful – Portugal had gone on to win 3–2 – and not because of any faith the manager had in him.

After losing their first game, England knew that they couldn't afford any further slip-ups. A far from vintage Germany side had not been at their best in a 1–1 draw with Romania, and they were still reliant on players whose best days were behind them, such as Lothar Matthäus.

At 39, the veteran sweeper was almost twice as old as Owen, and set to win his 150th cap against England; Matthäus had won his first cap in 1980, when Owen was just six months old. It was hoped that the Liverpool youngster's pace would prove incisive against the creaking legs of the German legend.

Keegan again mixed praise for Owen with some tough talk regarding Owen's disappointing first half in the match. 'Hopefully, we'll get the right reaction from him,' the coach said, 'but, if he plays for 45 minutes like that again in a game as big as that, then we will have to change things again.'

Owen made it through the interval without being replaced and even had a hand in the opening goal eight minutes after the break. He flicked on a Beckham free kick and Shearer headed home for the only goal of the game. Soon after, however, Keegan sent on Owen's young Liverpool teammate Steven Gerrard in his place to strengthen the midfield, a sensible and successful tactical in a must-win game, but another blow to the young striker's confidence.

The third group game saw England tackle Romania, against whom Owen had come on with devastating effect in France two years before. Dan Petrescu, the Romania hero of that night in Toulouse, had not forgotten the impact the player had made. 'We all remember Owen, because in that game in Toulouse he came on against us and was England's best player, even though he was only on the pitch for 15 minutes. We know how fast Owen can be but now we have a tactic to stop him, if he plays.'

If he plays. Owen's place in the team was by no means certain. But again Keegan went with him, and he rewarded his manager with a goal before half time that gave England a somewhat undeserved 2–1 lead. Owen was full of confidence, until he got into the changing room at half-time. Keegan congratulated his young attacker on the goal and then, in front of the rest of the squad, went on to tell him everything that he was doing wrong.

Romania grabbed a deserved equaliser three minutes after half-time, and Owen was again hauled off with the score at 2–2. As in the Portugal match, that scoreline eventually turned to 3–2 and England were out of the tournament. In truth, they had never looked like potential champions, apart from that opening 18 minutes against Portugal.

Shearer called time on his international career and Owen was keen to stake his claim as England's top striker. 'People say the scrutiny will be on me when Alan Shearer goes but, if that's the case, then I've got 20-odd caps and feel experienced enough to be able to deal with that. I've played in World Cup and now European Championship finals and I'm prepared. I'm not going to be running scared of it.'

Fortunately for Owen, he was still just 20 years old and had plenty of time to establish himself as England's first-choice striker. Keegan, however, would soon be out of work. His days as England boss were numbered.

7

The new season began in a flurry of transfer activity as Gerard Houllier looked to build on the fourth-placed finish in the league the previous year. In came German wing-back Christian Ziege from Middlesbrough, midfielder Nick Barmby from Everton, Borussia Dortmund's veteran defender Markus Babbel and the experienced Scot Gary McAllister from Coventry. McAllister turned out to be the most influential signing, as his cool head helped to control many a game from midfield throughout Liverpool's long season. But it was notable that no more strikers would be joining the Anfield playing staff.

The capture of Emile Heskey midway through the previous campaign had swelled the attacking ranks on Merseyside and, alongside Robbie Fowler, Titi Camara and Michael Owen, it meant that competition for places upfront would continue to be fierce.

'We have to go into the season with plenty of confidence,' Owen said 'if only from looking around the club and seeing so many top players here from so many countries. I don't want to talk about titles or anything like that – we must get off to a good start and have better runs in cups because we certainly didn't do that last term. We must do well in Europe. It's going to be an exciting season and we intend to win some silverware.'

After three full seasons in the first team, Owen had developed a serious hunger for some cups and medals, and this would be the season that Liverpool finally stepped up on that front.

Houllier laughed off reports that Owen was on his way out of the club. 'I heard a rumour last night that Real Madrid were supposed to be in Liverpool,' Houllier said. 'I can understand that: it's a nice city for tourists! But as far as coming to visit our club, that's not happened. We've struggled to get Michael fit and back to what he used to be, and he is looking very close to it. Any transfer? No chance.'

At least one of his managers appreciated him: Owen was on the bench for England's first game in September, and it was clear that Kevin Keegan's opinion hadn't changed since Euro 2000. Liverpool's season began dramatically as they beat Bradford City 1–0 at Anfield, before losing 2–0 to Arsenal at Highbury in a match lit up by three red cards. And the Reds then surrendered a 3–0 lead at the Dell as they let Southampton rescue a point in a 3–3 draw.

Owen got the first and third goals against Glenn Hoddle's side and both strikes came courtesy of his left boot – a point he emphasised by pointing to his weaker foot after each goal. This strange celebration in front of his former international coach showed how much the criticism of the previous season had got to the normally self-assured goalscorer, but the improvement in his game wasn't enough to merit selection by Keegan for the friendly against France in Paris. But Owen replaced Scholes with 11 minutes to go, and the jilted striker grabbed an equaliser seven minutes later, volleying home Kieron Dyer's cross at the far post.

'I think I gave the perfect answer out there,' he told the press. 'I haven't become a bad player overnight.'

England faced Germany next, in the last game to be played at Wembley before the renovation work began, and they were desperate to get their World Cup qualifying campaign off to a good start. With only the top-placed team in the group certain of a place at the finals in Japan and Korea, Owen was committed to making sure it was England. 'It would be a sin,' the young forward insisted, 'for the players that we've got in our country not to be performing on the best stage.'

Owen and Andy Cole, the duo who had finished upfront together against France, started together against Germany. With 14 goals between them already – eight to Owen – as the season entered October, they were certainly the form men. But none of England's players rose to the occasion in the last game under the Twin Towers, and Germany went away with a deserved 1–0 win, courtesy of a Hamann free kick that skidded past David Seaman in the pouring rain. Keegan, amid emotional scenes, resigned after the game.

With only four days until England's next match the FA appointed Howard Wilkinson as caretaker manager for the game against Finland in Helsinki. The former Leeds boss showed as little faith in Owen as his predecessor and decided to recall Teddy Sheringham to play upfront with Cole. As the game petered out to a 0–0 draw, Wilkinson didn't even summon the in-form Owen from the bench.

His year went from bad to worse when a collision with

Derby defender Chris Riggott's knee opened up the back of the striker's head. The skin tore open and blood began to pour out from a wound that needed thirteen stitches to close. After being taken to hospital and stitched up, Owen insisted on a return to the ground so he could travel back to Liverpool on the team bus with the rest of the squad. But the effects of the blow were so bad that he then went to a Liverpool hospital, where he had two brain-scans and was kept in overnight for observation.

Owen suffered dizzy spells, which delayed his comeback, and in the three weeks that he was out, he missed five games. But Liverpool coped admirably with his absence, as Heskey hit six goals in four matches.

Owen returned in time to help Liverpool into the third round of the UEFA Cup with a 3–2 win over Liberec, setting up a tie with Olympiakos. Owen was forced off with a recurrence of his back injury in the first leg and was left on the bench for the second leg, but goals from Heskey and Barmby helped the Reds to a 2–0 win.

Heskey had firmly established himself as Houllier's first choice upfront, with 12 goals in 12 games, and Owen was now left to battle it out with Fowler for a place alongside the former Leicester striker. And it was obvious that neither of Liverpool's home-grown shooting stars would be happy on the bench.

Owen said, 'I don't just say I'm the best because that is what's expected, I believe it. I have to, because there is no other way you can survive at the top. I know Robbie is the same. I really believe in my ability and that I should be playing. I am sure everyone understands that desire, because it is the one that drives you.'

Liverpool entered 2001 in fifth place in the Premiership and, as the transfer window opened across the European leagues, Houllier took the opportunity to bolster his squad further. The Finnish striker Jari Litmanen joined on a free transfer from Barcelona, and Owen had even more competition for his place in the team.

He was the victim of squad rotation for the first time in his career and it appeared to contribute to his rustiness in the League Cup semi-final, where Owen missed a couple of chances in the first leg against Crystal Palace. In a 2–1 defeat at Selhurst Park the young star was well below his best, and he was relegated to the bench for the next two games.

Another hamstring injury then flared up, ruling him out of the League Cup semi-final second leg, but Liverpool battered the Eagles 5–0 without him. Houllier's solid defence and rapid counterattacking style had seemed well suited to cup football, and so it was proved as the Reds were on their way to Cardiff with hopes of a first trophy since 1995.

Before the League Cup final Owen had plenty of time to get back to form and fitness and, as well as a playing for a place in the team for the final, he received extra motivation with news from FA headquarters. The men in charge at Soho Square had spent four months searching for the right man for the job, and they thought they'd found him in a Swedish former Benfica, Sampdoria and Lazio boss. Sven-Göran Eriksson was named as Keegan's full-time successor, and Owen was keen to impress the man who had been one of his long-term admirers.

With the great sense of timing that had shone through

when he was at his best, Owen found the perfect game to dazzle, as he scored both goals in a 2–0 win over Roma in the Olympic Stadium, a month after Eriksson took control, and with the Swede watching from the stands. It was a great boost for Liverpool – in the very stadium in which they had clinched their European Cup wins in 1977 and 1984 – and his manager was delighted. 'I knew a week ago he was back to his best,' Houllier said. 'In training and against Sunderland last week he looked sharp and very lively. When he is like that he is always a threat and can score goals. I was very pleased with his performance.'

The next game for Liverpool was in the FA Cup as Houllier's side continued their four-pronged quest for trophies, and Owen was left out as Heskey and Litmanen put Manchester City to the sword. Missing an FA Cup fifth-round tie was of little consequence to Owen, since he was by now well used to being left out; but a week later he found himself on the bench for the League Cup final, and that remains one of his biggest footballing disappointments. Liverpool beat Birmingham City on penalties, but Owen found little satisfaction in his winner's medal.

There was no time for him to dwell on his disappointment, however, as England faced Spain three days later in Eriksson's first game in charge. Owen was delighted to be picked for his first game, and this faith from the start established the foundations for what was to prove a good working relationship between the young striker and his new international coach.

Like the four previous managers before him, the Swede started his tenure as England boss with a win and the players, press and fans were happy with the new man. A

3–0 win over the dangerous Spaniards was a great result, and, although Owen didn't get among the goals, he still did enough to prove himself worthy of selection.

Liverpool continued to struggle in the league away from home, but they were having no such problems in the cups, and as they entered March the Reds were in the quarter-finals of the FA Cup and UEFA Cup, with the League Cup already in the bag. Thanks to Owen's goals they were swiftly into the semis of both competitions and Owen was confident that the treble was 'on'.

With two goals in two games, Owen was hitting top form at just the right time. The Reds had made themselves very difficult to beat, and with his pace and finishing there was always the chance of a goal. In short, Houllier had made his counterattacking team perfect for cup football.

England's first competitive match under Eriksson, against Finland, started badly as they fell behind to a Gary Neville own goal, but Owen equalised just before half-time and Beckham scored the winner, rewarding the manager's faith in giving him the captain's armband. Since they had claimed only one point from their first two qualifying games, the win over the Finns was vital to the England cause, as were another three points against Albania. Owen made it five goals in five games, grabbing his 10th for England in his 27th appearance for his country, as Eriksson's side won 3–1 in Tirana. The two victories helped to get the qualifying campaign back on track after a dismal start and, with three wins in his first three games, the new coach had started well.

March had been a fine month for Owen and it finished gloriously for Liverpool as they completed their first league double over Manchester United for over 22 years. Having already won at Old Trafford in December, the Reds won 2–0 at Anfield to send their fans home in raptures. Owen appeared for only the last two minutes, so it was of little surprise that he failed to get on the scoresheet for the first time in six games, but for once his goals weren't required as Gerrard and Fowler wrapped up a sweet victory.

April was far less fruitful for the 21-year-old, but Liverpool's trophy quest continued unabated. They made it into the UEFA Cup final after beating Barcelona 1–0 on aggregate, and it took two late goals from Heskey and Fowler to beat Wycombe Wanderers in the FA Cup semi-final at Villa Park.

Liverpool also picked up ten points from five Premiership games to keep them in contention for a Champions League place the following season, and, as the 2000-01 season drew to a close, it was clear that Owen and his teammates still had plenty to play for.

Owen showed once again that he could be relied upon to get goals when it mattered, by grabbing nine goals in six games in May, including an amazing cameo in the FA Cup Final against Arsenal on 12 May.

Liverpool were completely and utterly outplayed for most of the match at the Millennium Stadium, but came away with the famous old trophy, thanks to a late double from the Boy Wonder. Arsenal dominated for 80 minutes, but were unable to take their chances as the Liverpool defence stood firm once more. Fredrik Ljungberg finally got the breakthrough after 72 minutes, but the Gunners couldn't find a second to put the game beyond doubt.

The Reds hit back with a heavy psychological blow as

Owen hit an equaliser ten minutes later, McAllister's free-kick was knocked down by Babbel and Owen held off Keown to spin and knock the ball past David Seaman. Having worked so hard to get ahead, the Arsenal players' shoulders dropped as they began to think it might not be their day.

After the disappointment of missing out on the League Cup final, Owen was determined to make it his. Five minutes later Arsenal won a corner, but Liverpool cleared the danger and the ball fell to Patrik Berger, who sent a beautiful ball down the inside-left channel for Owen to run onto. Lee Dixon was back for the Gunners but Liverpool's No. 10 had too much pace for the old full-back, and Owen was past him in the blink of an eye. Tony Adams tried to get across, but Owen shot left-footed before his former England teammate could get to him, and the low strike bounced over Seaman's outstretched hand and into the bottom corner.

Jamie Carragher summed up his teammates' thoughts about Owen and his man-of-the-match performance. 'He is still only 21 and he will say himself that he is still learning the game, but he has proved without doubt that he has got what it takes. Against Arsenal he was the difference – and that difference was someone who can finish clinically. He had two chances and we won the game. He is a class act, a class finisher. The final showed what he can do.'

But there could be little celebration for Owen's unbelievable achievement, since there was still a UEFA Cup final and a final Premiership game to try to secure third place. Owen started his second cup final of the season, but was replaced after 79 minutes as the manager chose to strengthen the midfield. Houllier's side had taken an early lead against Alavés and were two up after 15 minutes, but the Spanish side pulled one back and it was 3–1 at half-time thanks to a McAllister penalty for a foul by the keeper on Owen.

Liverpool's defence had been superb all season so there seemed little chance of an Alavés comeback, but that's exactly what happened as Javi Moreno grabbed two in six minutes to draw his team level. Fowler made it 4–3 after 72 minutes and Jordi Cruyff headed a late, late leveller with a minute to go and the final went to extra time.

Owen was once again forced to watch from the sidelines as his teammates tried to settle a cup final in the added 30 minutes, and this time he didn't have to bear the agony of penalties, as the unfortunate Geli headed a McAllister free kick into his own net, winning the cup for Liverpool by a golden goal, 5–4.

Liverpool had won an incredible Treble of League Cup, FA Cup and UEFA Cup, but the season's main objective was yet to be secured. A place in the Champions League depended on a win against Charlton at The Valley in the last Premier League game of the season.

With the game goalless at half-time, the players received a serious talking to in the dressing room and came out for the second half with a fierce resolve to win 4–0, with Owen grabbing Liverpool's last goal of the season.

Houllier's side had proved they could beat anyone on their day and by finishing third in the Premiership they would have the chance to take on Europe's finest the following season. It was a great year for Liverpool and the Anfield faithful lined the streets as the team displayed their cups from their open-topped bus parade from the training ground at Melwood down to Albert Dock.

Owen finally had some medals to show for all his goals and promise but, despite his 16 league goals, Liverpool ended up 11 points behind champions Manchester United, and he was determined to close the gap the following year. 'The league title is what I want,' he said. 'Personally I'd want to win the league before trying to conquer Europe. The table never lies and Manchester United have shown they are among the best in Europe.'

He had scored 24 goals in his 46 appearances at club level in 2000-01, as well as three from five for England, but his season still wasn't finished. Owen still had a couple of games to play for his country before he could take a well-earned break.

Sven-Göran Eriksson's side had a World Cup qualifying match against Greece in Athens, which they prepared for by playing Mexico at Pride Park. Owen started both games but failed to score in either. Nevertheless, England won both games convincingly and the World Cup qualifying campaign was well under way.

8

'I joined the club when I was 11 and every year we all get excited and optimistic about the start of the season. But this season there is probably an inner belief that we can get closer to the champions and do well in the Champions League and in the two cup competitions. There is a real belief we can do better this season. It's not a hope, it's a conviction.'

So said Owen at the start of the 2001-02 season. Houllier brought in John Arne Riise from Monaco to replace Christian Ziege, and Jerzy Dudek to replace Sander Westerveld, and his team quickly added two more pieces of silverware to their already-bulging trophy cabinet, as they won the FA Community Shield and the European Super Cup. They also saw off FC Haka of Finland thanks to a Michael Owen hat-trick, in a Champions League qualifying-round tie to ensure their place amongst Europe's elite.

He began the league campaign in the same prolific form as he had ended the previous one, and was feeling fit and full of goals. 'I haven't felt a single twinge from my hamstrings for as long as I can remember. I've learned a lot about my body in the last few years and I know what I need to do to get the best out of it. As soon as one match is over, I start preparing for the next one. I have a massage and do warm-down exercises. Hopefully it will keep me injury-free for as long as possible.'

Liverpool's 3–2 win over Bayern Munich in the European Super Cup was invaluable preparation for Owen's next game for England – an incredible match against Germany that would go down in history.

Owen would face the same goalkeeper, Oliver Kahn, in both matches and, having worked out how to score against him in Monaco, he would carry the knowledge to good effect a week later.

'He's a very dominant keeper and makes himself look very big when he comes out to confront you,' Owen said after winning the Super Cup. 'I learned my lesson from that first chance. I know now not to try to put the ball past him high, he's so big. I do know that whoever plays for England will have to be really good finishers, because he's fantastic. I missed one chance and you don't often get a second opportunity. So when it came I was intent on playing the ball past him low, first time, and it worked.'

With 20 goals in his last 16 games for Liverpool, 16 of which had come in the last 10 games, the young striker was in the form of his life and, facing Germany on 1 September 2001, he delivered the performance of his life.

It was by no means the best German team of all time but, with Kahn in goal and Michael Ballack in midfield, there were two genuine world-class performers. Owen's Liverpool teammate Dietmar 'Didi' Hamann brought familiarity to the midfield, and the giant Carsten Jancker

Young Michael worked hard at school but it could never compete with his passion for football – he was soon fulfilling every schoolboy's dream by playing on the hallowed pitch at Wembley.

Owen made his Liverpool debut against Wimbledon in May 1997, coming on as a sub and scoring.

'That' goal! The unforgettable moment young Owen burst into the world's consciousness with a heart-stopping individual strike against Argentina in the 1998 World Cup.

While Owen slots home his hat-trick in the 5–1 drubbing of Germany in September 2001 (*top*), scores against Brazil in the 2002 World Cup (*left*), and in Euro 2004 against Portugal (*above*), England failed to deliver in any of the major tournaments between 1998 and 2006.

Signed to Real Madrid, Owen acquainted himself with the substitutes' bench but when given a run out, he was happy to get stuck in and prove his point by striking the back of the net, as seen here against Barcelona.

Back in England, Owen debuts at Newcastle United in September 2005, up front with ex-England partner Alan Shearer, Toon legend and the man whose formidable goal record Owen hoped to build on at St James's Park.

Back in familiar action for England after recovering from his foot injury, Owen played a full 90 minutes and grabbed a goal against the Reggae Boyz of Jamaica in a pre-World Cup 6–0 thrashing.

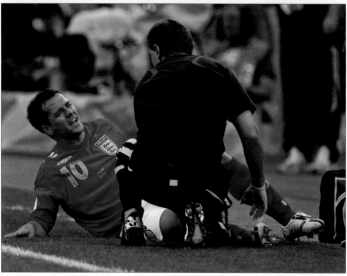

Disaster! After a 1–0 win in the second group game against Paraguay, fate struck a cruel blow again as Owen's cruciate knee ligament gave way against Sweden in the third World Cup game, spelling the end of his tournament and another long period out from the game he loves.

brought plenty of presence to the attack. And it was the big man who scored first, steering home a header from his strike partner Oliver Neuville after only six minutes.

But the home side's lead didn't last long and inevitably, with what was to follow, it was Owen who bagged the equaliser, seven minutes later. Owen and Heskey continued to scare the life out of the German defenders and they looked dangerous every time they had the ball. However, it was their Liverpool teammate Steven Gerrard who put England in front, hitting an unstoppable 25-yard pile driver just before the break. It was his first goal for England – and what a time to get it!

Just three minutes into the second half, Owen made it 3–1. Displaying all the understanding developed at club level, Heskey chested the ball down for his strike partner, and the little goal machine got there first to knock his second past Kahn. After 66 minutes he struck again, before Heskey wrapped up a fantastic night for England, and for Liverpool, with goal number five. It was only Germany's second defeat in 61 World Cup qualifying games and their first on home soil, but for England it was worth more than three points.

'This is the stuff dreams are made of,' Eriksson said afterwards. 'What can you say about Michael Owen? He took his goals brilliantly but this was a victory for the team and I would not like to pick one person out.'

To qualify for the tournament in Japan and South Korea, it was imperative that England remain focused for their next game four days later against Albania at St James' Park. Resolutely defending from start to finish, the Albanians were much more difficult to break down than

England's previous opponents, but it ended 2–0, thanks to a goal each from Owen and Fowler at the end of each half.

The six points from two games put Eriksson's side to the top of Group 9 with 16 points. They were now in control of their own destiny, having looked play-off hopefuls at best a week previously, and they knew that a win against Greece at Old Trafford in October would secure their place in the Far East. But Owen would play no part in the final group game, because he had suffered yet another hamstring injury.

Owen continued to be busy during this particular injury hiatus, as he signed a new contract extension for a further four years on a wage believed to be between £60,000 and £80,000 per week. As England lined up against Greece at Old Trafford, Owen watched the big game as a television analyst, trying to remain analytical as his teammates twice went behind and were dragged through to the World Cup by a monumentally inspirational captain's performance from Beckham, and his crucial last-minute free kick.

Ecstatic to have finally seen England's place at the World Cup confirmed, Owen could begin to think about building on the reputation he had laid the foundations for in St Etienne. But, in October, there was still plenty to play for at club level, where Liverpool were set to be without Gérard Houllier for much of the season.

Still recuperating from his latest hamstring trouble, Owen was merely a spectator at Anfield when Liverpool's French manager was rushed to hospital with a serious heart condition. As Owen watched from the directors' box, he noticed that the manager didn't appear for the second half, and spotted that Houllier's wife had also disappeared from her usual seat, but the true scale of the problem didn't come to light until the next day.

At training the players were told that the manager's condition was 'very serious and possibly life-threatening'. Houllier had a dissection of the aorta and required an 11-hour operation to fix the issue.

Everything was dedicated to the manager for the next five months. The family feel of the club was underlined by the way the fans reacted to the news that the man who had guided them through such a trophy-laden season the year before was now fighting for his life in a hospital bed: they chanted his name at matches, home and away, and unfurled a massive French flag with Houllier's name on it across the Kop.

Two months after the operation the manager began calling some of the players over the phone, and a couple of weeks after that he began regular visits to Melwood, never to do any work, but merely to stay in touch with the club and the players. It wasn't until five months later that Houllier finally reclaimed his spot on the Liverpool bench.

By the time he returned, Liverpool had been knocked out of both domestic cups and slipped from first to fourth in the table. Owen, though, had capped a fine year by picking up the European Footballer of the Year award, the Ballon d'Or, on a glittering night in Paris.

Only the sixth British player to win the award, Owen joined Sir Stanley Matthews, Denis Law, Sir Bobby Charlton, George Best and Kevin Keegan on an illustrious list. He was the first Englishman to pick up the trophy since 1979 and the first player in England to claim the 'golden ball' since 1968. For Owen, having only recently turned 22, it was incredible that he should find himself on a winner's list that included such greats as Franz Beckenbauer, Michel Platini and Johan Cruyff.

'I could not believe it when I first heard the news,' he said. 'I knew I was one of the five nominated but it was still a shock. There was Francesco Totti, Raúl and David Beckham and they are all fantastic footballers. We've had a great season for Liverpool, winning five trophies and I'm very happy to win this award too. It's the highest privilege I can win as a player and I'm over the moon to win it.'

And inevitably, the award aroused fresh approaches from Europe's top clubs. Real Madrid president Florentino Pérez said quite boldly, 'We want Michael Owen. Owen can be one of the world's great players and the best players must play for Real Madrid. In England there are two great players, Owen and Beckham, but Beckham plays in the same position as Luis Figo. With the signing of Zidane, many French people and Arabs became Real Madrid fans. Now I would like to sign an English star.'

Houllier returned to give his team talk before the Champions League semi-final against Bayer Leverkusen, but despite Owen giving Liverpool a 1–0 lead from the home leg, they went out of Europe after a 4–2 reverse in Germany.

After 84 minutes of the second leg, Houllier's side were level on aggregate and still ahead by virtue of their away-goals; but, on a night when everything that could go wrong did go wrong, Owen missed three chances that he would normally be expected to score, and the usually reliable defence conceded a late goal to see Liverpool dumped out of the competition.

Showing remarkable 'bouncebackability' after the

Champions League defeat, Owen and Liverpool dug deep against Sunderland to keep their title challenge on track, an Owen winner moving them to within one point of Arsenal at the top. 'We've got a lot of hard games left,' he said after securing an 11th win in 12 games. 'Tottenham away is never easy, and we've got three home games, but we have to win them all to stand any chance.'

However, before Owen could take any more steps towards what would be a first championship for Liverpool since 1990, he had more history to make with his other team. On 17 April 2002, he led out his country at Anfield to become England's youngest captain since Bobby Moore. With Beckham out of action because of a broken metatarsal, Eriksson turned to Owen. 'He was the best footballer in Europe last year,' Eriksson said, explaining his decision. 'And I think he's a very clean and popular one inside and outside England. It's up to him to show that he's also a leader, and I think he is.'

And Owen certainly wasn't understating what it meant to him. 'If you had asked me just a few hours ago to list ambitions,' the new skipper told reporters, 'being England captain would have been one of them. It's something I wanted as a child. I'd love to captain Liverpool, to play in a few World Cups, win a World Cup. Then there's the league title and European Cups. Everyone has their ambitions and being skipper of England was one of mine.'

Facing Paraguay in a final warm-up match at home before heading for the Far East, Owen didn't disappoint. He led from the front and opened the scoring after just four minutes, somewhat appropriately heading in a Gerrard cross in front of the Kop. England went on to win the game

4–0 and Owen had completed a far better job than the last time he had led out his country, having been sent off against Yugoslavia while wearing the armband at Under-18s level.

Derby were the visitors to Anfield as the history-making forward claimed a brace to win the game 2–0, and consign the Rams to relegation. The three points had a more invigorating effect on Liverpool, however, since they lifted the Reds to the top of the table. Arsenal, though, were just two points behind with two games in hand. With three games left, Owen remained focused on the task at hand. 'We still feel we can win the title and that has to be the next target,' he said. 'Arsenal have the games in hand, but if they slip up then we're there waiting, and they know that. That puts on its own pressures.'

But it was Liverpool who couldn't handle the pressure, and losing 1–0 to Tottenham at White Hart Lane effectively ended their title dreams; and, when Wenger's team then beat Bolton, Liverpool's title was a mathematical impossibility.

'I still think that it's been a good season,' Owen reflected. 'The points total we ended up with could probably win the league next year. That shows just how far we've come. We have such a young side and have grown up together, and I don't think the manager will change things drastically in the summer. He might buy one or two players – but that's in his hands.'

Liverpool clearly needed someone to share the goalscoring burden. Owen's 28 goals gave him more than double those of the Reds' next-best marksman, Heskey, who got 13. But, despite Owen's obvious importance to his club, his country and his position as European Footballer of the Year, he still missed out on selection for

the Professional Footballers' Association Premiership team of the season, where his peers paired Thierry Henry and Ruud van Nistelrooy upfront. 'I don't want to be bitter but, if it had been picked at the start of the year, I would have been in it because of the start I had and the goals against Germany and Albania,' Owen said. 'Players pick for the moment and, at the time they voted, Ruud van Nistelrooy, Robert Pires, Thierry Henry and Craig Bellamy were on fire.'

He may have been underappreciated by his fellow pros, but Owen would have the support of the whole country for the next month and a half as England headed out East for the World Cup.

9

Due to the ever-increasing popularity of the Premiership in Japan, England arrived at their World Cup base amid an incredible amount of attention, from press and public alike. It was unlike anything Owen had ever seen before, and, although he didn't create as much frenzy among the locals as David Beckham, the Liverpool lad was clearly the second most popular of the England players with the Japanese public.

After Owen's anticlimactic end to the season, he could feel the pressure to succeed increasing day by day. 'Obviously, everyone wants England to do well and wants the players to play well, so there's an expectancy, but if you're a footballer that's what you're paid to do,' Owen said. 'I'm four years older, four years wiser, and it's going to be a great tournament. Hopefully, we can come out doing well. There's quite a lot of experience, even though we're a young side. We've got players from Manchester United, Arsenal, Liverpool who have all done well in Europe and who have all played in massive games before, so I don't think the stage will frighten any of the players.'

One of the players who would be missing out on the big stage was Owen's long-time teammate Steven Gerrard. The two had progressed through the Liverpool youth ranks together, and were now both key players in the England side, but the midfielder was going to miss the tournament due to a troublesome groin injury that required surgery. 'He's one of the best players in the world, let alone in England, and every team would miss him,' Owen said of Gerrard. 'It's a bitter blow because he would have had something to give on the world stage.'

But in the build-up to the tournament the British media had been more concerned with another injury, as the whole nation was gripped by metatarsal madness. Beckham had broken the second metatarsal in his left foot in Manchester United's 3–2 win against Deportivo la Coruña. Beckham's clubmate Gary Neville suffered a similar injury even closer to the tournament and was ruled out, and Danny Murphy was called up as a replacement before he too broke a metatarsal in training.

Following a relaxed week in Dubai with their partners, Eriksson's elite headed to South Korea for some hard graft. Training in the mornings and the evenings so as to avoid the heat of the day, they stepped up their preparation with friendly games against South Korea and Cameroon to ready themselves for the big kick-off. With Beckham still out, Owen continued as captain for the game against the co-hosts.

With many players looking ahead to the bigger game, the match against South Korea petered out to a 1–1 draw, despite Owen opening the scoring midway through the first half. The captain turned in a rebound after Paul Scholes

shot from distance to make it two goals from two matches with the armband.

England's first group game was against Sweden, a side they hadn't beaten since 1968, and, having played against most of the Swedish side in the Premiership, Owen knew exactly what to expect. 'The first game against Sweden is massive, and we can't afford to be beaten,' Owen told the press. 'If we are, we would have to win our other two matches, against Nigeria and Argentina, and that would be asking an awful lot.'

England took the lead 23 minutes into the game against Eriksson's homeland, as Sol Campbell headed home Beckham's corner. But the longer the game went on, the further back the defence of Danny Mills, Rio Ferdinand, Campbell and Ashley Cole dropped to defend David Seaman's goal and the lead. There were far too many long balls forward for Owen and Darius Vassell to chase, and Sweden got a deserved equaliser just before the hour mark. England retreated further and further into their own half, inviting the pressure onto them, and in the end they did well to hold on for a 1–1 draw.

Argentina had beaten Nigeria 1–0 in their opening game and were thus first in Group F, but if England could beat the Albicelestes in their next game, it would put them on top of their mini-table. The players needed no extra motivation ahead of arguably the biggest game of the entire group stage.

A rerun of their classic encounter in 1998, with some of the same characters, the game in Sapporo gave Beckham a chance to get revenge over Diego Simeone, and the rest of the players the chance to erase their spot-kick agony.

'Certain things like that rest in the memory,' Owen said, recalling St Etienne. 'It would be nice to beat them and get our own back. We can beat Argentina – on our day we can beat any team in the world.'

The build-up to the game also centred on England's other World Cup meeting with the South Americans, when Diego Maradona robbed Bobby Robson's side of a place in the World Cup semi-finals in 1986. The Argentinians were stereotyped as cunning, and Owen was asked to what extent he would bend the rules in pursuit of victory. 'I don't think you should cheat but you should be clever,' the Liverpool striker told reporters. 'If you go down without being touched that's cheating. But, if you can try to make someone foul you by enticing someone to get a toe in and they bring you down, then that's not cheating. That's drawing a foul. If some clumsy defender wants to throw himself in front of you, what are you going to do? Let him do it?'

Sure enough, just before half-time Owen was tripped for a penalty and Beckham made no mistake from the spot. Television replays suggested that Owen had dived but, running towards goal, he knocked the ball past the defender and invited the challenge. A gash in Owen's leg showed there was certainly enough contact to warrant a penalty. The nerves were visible as Beckham strode up to put the ball on the spot, and the relief was palpable as he smashed the ball down the middle of the goal and into the net. Afterwards Owen revealed that he had offered to take the kick for his captain, but was rebuffed. 'I asked David if he fancied it and he was really up for it,' the striker said. 'I could see that he was nervous, but at the same time it was important for him to do it – and I knew that.'

The rest of the game was marked by England's superb defensive effort and steely resolve and they held out to win 1–0 and go second on goal difference, Sweden having beaten Nigeria earlier in the day. 'It was a vital victory but it will only mean anything if we go on and beat Nigeria,' Owen said.

But having worked hard to reach that position, Eriksson's side laboured in the heat and humidity to draw 0–0 in their final group game against Nigeria. 'The only positive thing to take from the game is that we're through,' a pragmatic Owen told the press. 'But from now on we know we have to win every game, so we need better performances, and I'm sure they will be.

Eriksson was equally unfazed by the lack of goals from his number-one striker. 'I don't think Michael is disappointed. I think he's happy and is playing better and better. He is becoming sharper,' stated the England coach. 'Of course, we hope that he starts scoring again and he will do that. I shouldn't be at all surprised if his next goal comes at the weekend.'

Right on cue, Owen grabbed his first of the World Cup against the Danes. Eriksson kept faith with the same 11 who had disappointed so spectacularly against Nigeria, and this time they did him proud. Rio Ferdinand opened the scoring with a header and Owen made it 2–0 five minutes later. Butt flicked on a cross from Sinclair and the Liverpool striker got clear of the Danish defence to slide the ball left-footed past the keeper.

Heskey added a third just before the break, but there was anxiety as Owen came off at half time with a groin injury. In the post-match press conference he put a brave face on things, but he knew he was in trouble. 'I could have stayed on, I think,' he said. 'I felt something in my groin after a couple of minutes. I haven't had any groin problems before, so I wasn't sure what it was. I played on for 45 minutes, but when we went 3–0 up I thought there was no point in carrying on and leaving yourself exposed to get an injury for the next game. It was a precautionary type thing and if the scoreline had been goalless then I would have probably carried on.'

It was a sensible decision. Next up was Brazil, and England would need their speedy striker if they were to stand any chance against the tournament favourites.

Midway through the first half, Owen used all his experience in front of goal to pounce on a mistake by Lúcio. Heskey put a ball over the top and the defender was too busy concentrating on Owen to pick up the flight of the ball, so, as it dropped in behind the unfortunate centre-back, the Liverpool striker was already onto it and bearing down on the keeper.

Even with his injury Owen had too much pace for the defender to reach him, and he chipped Marcos and the ball nestled into the back of the net. It was 1–0 to England in the quarterfinal of the World Cup, and the fans began to believe that this really could be the year that the inventors of football reclaimed the sport's greatest trophy.

But it wasn't to be: just before the break Ronaldinho ran hard and fast through the middle of the England team, brushing off Ashley Cole, before laying the ball off for Rivaldo's sweet finish. If the defence had remained firm until the interval, it might have been a different story, but conceding so close to half-time had a huge psychological effect. England no longer looked like winners, and four minutes into the second half they were behind.

Again, it was the genius of Ronaldinho that left England reeling, as he lobbed Seaman with a free kick from 40 yards; and, although the buck-toothed entertainer was sent off for a tackle on Mills in the 57th minute, the damage was already done. Playing with a one-man advantage, Eriksson's side still looked clueless, pumping long ball after long ball forward, more in hope than expectation. It was a sad end to a tournament that had promised so much for an incredibly talented squad, but the Brazilians held on easily for a 2–1 win and England were on their way home.

'We've got to take as many positive things out of this as we can and move forward in four years time,' said Owen. 'You can't play at your maximum all the time and I'm glad to be part of such a good side. We're all looking forward to the future.'

With four more years' experience and a fully fit squad, England would be among the contenders at the next World Cup, and Owen thought that the absence of one of his teammates was felt particularly strongly in Japan and South Korea. 'Of course, we missed Steven Gerrard. He could have made a difference for us. He is a great player now and will be an even better one in the future but this time it just wasn't to be.'

Brazil went on to win the World Cup, beating a stubborn Turkey side in the semi-finals and a fairly average German side in the final. Once again, for England it was a case of 'if only'.

10

Michael Owen did a lot of growing up in the 2002-03 season. As well as enjoying the birth of his first child, the Liverpool star had to deal with a new Boy Wonder coming onto the England scene and the revelations about his gambling debts making a splash in the national newspapers. He also managed to rid himself, finally, of the persistent hamstring troubles that had afflicted him for the previous two and a half years.

Owen's penchant for gambling made him the subject of gossip up and down the country after one of the Sunday papers found out that he had allegedly written a £30,000 cheque to England teammate Kieron Dyer. Over a five-week period in Dubai, South Korea and Japan, Owen played cards with Dyer, Teddy Sheringham, David James and Wayne Bridge, apparently running up quite a debt.

With another report alleging that over a two-and-a-half year period he had staked a total of £2.2 million with various firms, the millionaire footballer came out to defend his clean-cut image and deny accusations of a gambling addiction. 'I fully accept that high-profile sports people like me are role models for youngsters and I would never encourage anyone to gamble,' Owen said. 'I've done nothing wrong. I can't believe some of the hurtful allegations that have been thrown at me, especially as they're so obviously inaccurate. I would never deliberately do anything to embarrass my club, my country, myself and, most importantly, my family.'

But, as a horse owner and fan of racing, Owen would continue to enjoy a flutter on the gee-gees. 'This publicity will not stop my love for horses,' he added. 'They're my main hobby outside of football.'

Long before the furore over his betting broke across the tabloids, Owen had enjoyed a mixed start to the season. Liverpool made it to November before suffering a domestic defeat, but the normally prolific striker made it to the end of September before scoring a goal in open play. Gérard Houllier had strengthened the squad considerably after the World Cup, bringing in Senegalese duo El Hadji Diouf and Salif Diao and the French midfielder Bruno Cheyrou for a combined fee of £19 million. Diouf was the African Player of the Year and had impressed at the World Cup, helping Senegal into the quarter-finals on their World Cup debut.

Milan Baros also arrived from Banik Ostrava. Having initially signed for the Reds midway through the previous season, the 20-year-old striker had continued to play in the Czech Republic until a work permit could be acquired. With new additions to the front line, Houllier decided not to extend the loan deal that had brought Nicolas Anelka to Anfield, and he also allowed Jari Litmanen to return to his old club Ajax.

To banish his injury problems once and for all, Owen began a series of strengthening exercises on his damaged hamstrings to build them back up to the level they were at before his initial tear at Elland Road in April 1999. On top of all the normal pre-season training, he did a lot of extra work on his legs, and, when the season started with the FA Community Shield, he was clearly not at his best.

Liverpool lost 1–0 to Double winners Arsenal in Cardiff, and although the Reds began their competitive season solidly there were few goals from the usually prolific Owen. He even missed a penalty in the game against Aston Villa.

As an obvious problem with the rotation system came to light, Owen sulkily sat out the 2–0 defeat to Valencia in Spain. He returned to the team for the Anfield match against West Bromwich Albion, but he wasn't enjoying the rub of the green in the autumn of 2002 and he bungled his second spot kick of the season, to increase the talk of his demise.

Sami Hyypia was quick to defend his teammate. 'Michael was very unlucky on Saturday. He missed the penalty and a couple of other chances and I really felt sorry for him. He's going through a period where the goals aren't going in at the moment but he'll soon turn things around. Everyone in the squad will help him get through this spell.'

The rehabilitation had taken its toll on Owen and he wasn't as sharp as usual on the pitch, but as his extra training eased off a level the England attacker was soon back to his best. He didn't score in the Champions League draw with FC Basel but, after four minutes of the Premiership clash against Manchester City, Owen scored a first goal of the season from open play.

In typical Owen style, he followed it up with plenty more, as he grabbed a hat-trick in the 3–0 win at Maine Road, and the European Footballer of the Year was back to his goalscoring best. His celebrations, especially that for the third goal, belied the calm face he put on things afterwards when asked about his drought. 'The truth is there was not much wrong,' Owen said. 'I wasn't unduly happy about the way I'd been playing. Of course, the thing that was missing was goals. But I've been through spells like this before and I will again. I knew how to deal with it. The most important thing was my self-confidence stayed intact. I don't think I'll ever lose that.'

Liverpool beat Spartak Moscow 5–0 at Anfield to help steady their European course in Group B of the Champions League, before Owen continued his return to form with the only goal of the game at home to Chelsea. The win took Houllier's side to within two points of Arsenal at the top of the table, since the Gunners had started the season in the same phenomenal form as they had finished the last one. But, despite Owen's early lack of form, Liverpool had almost matched the Champions, and with the little man back to his best it was hoped they could really challenge the Londoners for the title.

Points were just as important for England when Owen joined his international colleagues for the start of their Euro 2004 qualifying campaign. Eriksson could count himself lucky that Owen had played his way back to form at club level, when his No. 10 scored the winner after 82 minutes. England went behind to Slovakia after 24 minutes, but Beckham equalised with a free-kick before the Liverpool striker's goal spared England's blushes late on.

The match was marred by racist abuse directed at England's black players, and scuffles in the crowd, and Slovakia proved to be a very hostile environment for Owen and his teammates as they heard gunshots from their hotel

through the night, but they returned home with three valuable points and faced Macedonia at Southampton's St Mary's Stadium four days later in another qualifier.

England were a shambles on the south coast and not even Owen could rescue a win against the Balkan side. Following David Seaman's error in the World Cup, he allowed an Artim Sakiri corner to float over his head and into the far corner of the goal without anyone else touching it. Eriksson's side fought back from a goal behind twice to draw 2–2, but Seaman's treatment after the game left quite an impression. The unfair abuse and ridicule that the formerly great keeper got in the fallout from what proved to be his final international game astounded Owen, and in time it will be interesting to see whether the young striker calls time on his own international career rather than face the possibility of being hounded out by media and public persecution.

Back at club level, Liverpool maintained their hounding of Arsenal with a 1–0 win over Leeds in Yorkshire without Owen, before the hit man returned to grab his second hat-trick of the season in Russia. Spartak Moscow took a shock lead midway through the first half, but Owen's treble meant that the Reds won 3–1 and were now second in Group B with seven points from four games.

Owen got another important goal for Houllier as they returned to league action with a 2–1 win over Tottenham. It took an 86th-minute penalty from the in-form youngster to beat Spurs but he could do nothing to stop Valencia completing a double over his side with a 1–0 win at Anfield four days later. Rafa Benítez's team had embarrassed Liverpool in the Mestella six weeks previously on their way to a 2–0 win, and the humiliation was completed thanks to Francisco Rufete's shot, which deflected in off Hyypia.

Owen helped Liverpool to recover quickly from the defeat with two more goals against West Ham the following Sunday, as the Reds kept their title challenge on track. It took Owen's tally to 10 goals from his last seven starts, and made a mockery of the early-season criticism that he had had to put up with.

Liverpool saw their way past Southampton in the League Cup without Owen, before making the trip to Middlesbrough, where their unbeaten start to the league season came to an end. Having won nine and drawn three of their opening 12 matches, the Liverpool players were starting to believe this could be their year. The fans were, too. But Dudek made a huge mistake for the only goal of the game and, by the time leaves were back on the trees, the Reds' title dreams were gone. After all of their excellent early-season form, Houllier's side failed to win any of their next 11 Premiership matches.

It wasn't just their domestic form that suffered, however, as Liverpool found themselves out of the Champions League and into the UEFA Cup after they failed to beat FC Basel.

The UEFA Cup provided some welcome respite for Liverpool in the poor run of form as they saw off Vitesse Arnhem with 1–0 wins home and away, courtesy of Owen's goals, but in their league things remained dour. A 0–0 draw at home to Sunderland was followed by defeats to Fulham, Manchester United at home, Charlton and Sunderland.

'The main thing that is affected when you are on a run likes ours is your confidence,' Owen told reporters. 'Players are afraid to try anything for fear of making a mistake and sometimes even finding one of your own players with a

simple pass becomes difficult. Sometimes you are wary of launching an attack in case it breaks down and you concede at the other end. It is not physical or anything to do with a lack of ability. It is very much a mental thing.'

Liverpool beat Manchester City 1–0 in the third round of the FA Cup to lift spirits, but their form was still patchy as they lost their League Cup semi-final first leg 2–1 away to Sheffield United and then drew 1–1 with Aston Villa at Anfield. Owen got the goal that provided the Reds with their first point of 2003, and the following Saturday they beat Southampton away to record a first Premiership win for more than two months.

It was then that Owen's gambling debts came to light. Owen kept his head down and remained focused on scoring goals for Liverpool, and in their next game the occasional gambler hit the jackpot as his extra-time strike took the Reds to Cardiff for the League Cup final.

Houllier clearly felt that he owed his striker for the horrible memory of two years before. 'The last time we reached the Worthington Cup final Michael was in the dugout, so he deserves to play now,' the manager said. 'His attitude was brilliant that day. I will always remember when Jamie Carragher scored the winning penalty: Michael was jumping up, celebrating and punching the air. That tells you something about him.'

Liverpool drew 0–0 with Crystal Palace at Selhurst Park in the fourth round of the FA Cup, and were confident of beating the underdogs back at Anfield. But the Reds succumbed 2–0 in the replay and were left with just the UEFA Cup and the League Cup to hope for as trophies. In the Premiership, their stuttering form had left them well off the pace.

Owen saw his record as England's youngest-ever debutant beaten by Wayne Rooney in a friendly against Australia, a game Eriksson's side lost 3–1 after making 11 substitutions at half-time, Rooney among them. 'I can see similarities in our reputations,' Owen said of his new international teammate, 'but not similarities as players. He's probably more mature physically than I am now and he's probably got more hair on his chest – and I'm 23!'

Owen played only forty-five minutes against the Australians, but it was still another game without a goal, and the criticism was building up once again. 'I would be lying if I told you all this leaves me indifferent,' he revealed to the press. 'I'd like to be more consistent, and I have to be.'

His latest barren spell lasted only a month, and Owen once again hit top form after grabbing one goal. The breakthrough strike came in a 2–1 defeat away to Birmingham, and Owen scored again in the next game to register his 20th European goal for Liverpool. His strike in the 2–0 win over Auxerre secured his club's progress into the quarter-finals of the UEFA Cup, and equalled Ian Rush's Liverpool record.

In the next round Liverpool would face Celtic, the side against whom Owen scored his first European goal, and the team that most of his father's side of the family support. 'It's great to have equalled Ian Rush's record, very pleasing,' the striker told the press. 'Anything can happen now. As soon as we came out of the Champions League we fancied that we could do well in this competition. Now a tie against Celtic is a dream for us. I remember playing there when I was 17 in 1997. I scored and I'll remember that game for the rest of my life. I hope we can experience that atmosphere again.'

Owen's next game was at one of his other favourite grounds, as Liverpool faced Manchester United in the League Cup final in Cardiff. Playing at the Millennium Stadium brought Owen a new happy memory from the country he'd lived in all his life as he scored another late goal to win some silverware. Five minutes from time he struck the ball past Fabien Barthez to make it 2–0 and effectively end the game and guarantee a trophy in what was fast becoming a disappointing season.

'Certain grounds give you a buzz – and the Millennium Stadium is a lucky ground for us,' Owen said after the game. 'I scored twice here when we won the FA Cup against Arsenal a couple of years ago and that was my greatest moment in football. The atmosphere here is incredible. It's a very special place and I'm delighted we've made it even more special with this win.'

Still intent on securing a Champions League place, Liverpool went on a run of seven wins out of their next eight games in the league, but lost 3–1 on aggregate to Martin O'Neill's resilient Celtic side to go out of the UEFA Cup. A 4–0 thrashing at Old Trafford was the only defeat in a determined finish to the Premier League season, and Owen was scoring for fun again.

He took his goalscoring form to the international stage, grabbing the second goal in England's 2–0 win in Liechtenstein to help give the qualifying campaign a much-needed boost after the dismal 2–2 draw with Macedonia. The victory closed the gap to Group 7 leaders Turkey to two points and, with England's next game against the World Cup semi-finalists, they were still in a strong position.

Owen lined up alongside Rooney for the first time in the big match at Sunderland's Stadium of Light, and, although he went off after an hour with a back injury and the scores still level, his 17-year-old partner impressed everyone in his full debut as England beat the Turks 2–0.

There was no trouble finding the goal for Owen at club level, however, and, although Charlton kept him quiet as Liverpool won 2–1, the young striker marked the start of a memorable week with four goals in a 6–0 win over West Brom. Owen's second was his hundredth Premiership goal for the Reds and he dedicated the impressive haul to his soon-to-be-born baby. 'Louise is expecting to give birth on Thursday,' the centurion said. 'And by our next match I'll probably be a dad, so the ball will be a nice present for the new arrival.

'It's a great honour to join players like Ian Rush, Kenny Dalglish and Roger Hunt. I'm told Hunt has the all-time record of 245 League goals for the club. I'm not thinking about that now.'

Owen was more concerned with the impending arrival, and on Thursday, 1 May 2003, Gemma Rose Owen was born at Countess of Chester Hospital, the hospital where both the infant's mother and father had been born, in the very same maternity ward.

'This is the most amazing moment of my life,' Owen told the press. 'I think I was more nervous than Louise. We're very proud parents and look forward to spending time together as a family.'

Making a rare public statement, Louise was quoted as

saying, 'This is the happiest day of my life. I'm very tired but delighted. Gemma is absolutely gorgeous.' Owen had rushed from training to be at her bedside but his new baby's excellent sense of timing meant that he didn't need to skip any matches.

A couple of weeks after Gemma was born, Owen spoke more freely about life as a father. 'People have asked me to compare it to scoring a goal, but Gemma's birth came with an excitement unlike anything I've ever known. I'm not ashamed to say I shed a few tears. In fact I'm proud to say it.

'We were praying for her to arrive on time without being induced because of my heavy football commitments. It's only just starting to sink in for me. I get home from training and realise I have a new baby waiting for me. It's a fantastic feeling. I've watched Louise changing nappies and I've been trying to get the hang of it. It looks a bit technical for me at the moment, but after a few viewing sessions I reckon I'll be ready for it.'

But, with two games left of the league season, Owen's technical prowess was still needed on the pitch, where Liverpool were desperately chasing fourth place and a chance to play in the Champions League the following season. Their hopes were knocked by losing to Manchester City at home, and they headed to Stamford Bridge for the final game, knowing only a win would be good enough to get them into fourth.

Liverpool and Chelsea were level on 64 points from 37 games, so it was a winner-takes-all clash with a potential jackpot of £20 million for the victor. Despite going ahead through Hyypia, Houllier's side eventually lost 2–1 and would have to play in the UEFA Cup the following season.

They had finished fourth, third and then second in successive seasons, but there was to be no league title to complete the run in 2003. Instead Liverpool were fifth, a massive 19 points behind Manchester United.

Owen's form had fluctuated throughout the season from red-hot to ice-cold, and, although he matched his best-ever total with 28 goals – 19 in the Premiership, seven in Europe and two in the League Cup – he was disappointed with the ones that got away. Nevertheless, his fitness was clearly benefiting from the extra weights training, as Owen played in 54 matches for Liverpool and six for England between August and May, but his season still wasn't over.

On 11 June 2003, a month after the end of the season, Owen again led out England wearing the captain's armband, but this time the opponents were Slovakia, and the 23-year-old Liverpool striker was winning his 50th cap. His appearance made history on two counts, since he became his country's youngest ever captain in a competitive match, and beat the previous record of the youngest Englishman to a half-century of caps by two years. Owen wore the honour well, and claimed two goals to turn around the game, winning 2–1 after going behind.

The three points maintained a gap of two points between England and group leaders Turkey, but with England's game in hand they knew that two victories and then a draw in Istanbul would take them to the European Championship. It was a healthy position to be in, going into what would be a very short summer break for Owen, who had just ten days off before pre-season started.

11

The Liverpool season had once again started in hope and expectation, and Gérard Houllier had made further additions to his already impressive squad. Steve Finnan and Harry Kewell joined from Fulham and Leeds respectively but by far the most significant transfer of the summer as far as Owen was concerned was the one that took David Beckham from Manchester United to Real Madrid. As Beckham's vice-captain at international level, Owen was interested to see how 'Golden Balls' fared in La Liga, having previously spoken of a desire to expand his horizons.

Liverpool's German international Dietmar 'Didi' Hamann had spoken to Owen about the merits of playing abroad, and the England hero had taken it all on board. 'You would definitely broaden your experience by going abroad,' he said. 'There are plenty of options there for me. I don't think there are many players these days who would stay at a club from the age of 11 – like I was when I joined Liverpool – to the age of 35.'

With Owen's competitive edge, it would be only a

matter of time before he tested himself in a foreign environment, unless the Reds matched his trophy aspirations. 'If Liverpool are winning the League every year, there won't be any decision to be made,' he said. 'I am moving into a new house soon and all my family are close by. I have lived there all my life. You don't just jump up and go. I am happy at the moment. If we are a successful team, I will always be happy.'

Having scored 12 goals in the last 15 games of the previous season, Owen carried his success into the new season, but Liverpool's form was more varied. The Reds lost to Roman Abramovich's new Chelsea on the opening day of the season, despite Owen scoring his first of the season with a twice-taken penalty, and they drew their next two games 0–0.

In England's first game of the new campaign, Owen added to his international tally in the friendly win over Croatia. But before Eriksson's side played again the Liverpool striker helped his club to their first win of the season, scoring twice at Goodison Park as they beat Everton 3–0. 'I didn't have a good record in the derby until the last couple of years,' Owen said afterwards. 'So it's nice to score today, especially here.'

With the Reds' poor start to the season, and their continued reliance on Owen's goals, newspaper talk also turned to his impending contract negotiations. With only two seasons left on his existing deal, Liverpool were keen to sign their talented striker to a longer contract rather than see him walk away as a free agent.

Owen continued his pursuit of goals and records with a further strike against Charlton, but Liverpool went down

3–2 at the Valley and followed that with a 2–1 loss to Arsenal at Anfield. His latest goalscoring run had come to an end, but, worse than that, the prolific striker had picked up a shin injury with only a week to go until England's trip to Istanbul for their Euro 2004 qualifier. Ironically, Owen hurt himself tackling his international teammate Ashley Cole, and he had to watch on television as Eriksson's team qualified for the big tournament without him.

England had survived Owen's absence but things were different at club level, as Liverpool stuttered their way through the next three months with few appearances from the former European Footballer of the Year. The dodgy Premiership form increased the fears that Liverpool would miss out on Champions League football again, and talk once again turned to Owen's potential departure.

Interest from Spain followed with Real Madrid and Barcelona both making their intentions clear. The Nou Camp boss Frank Rijkaard broadcast his opinion on Spanish radio, saying, 'Owen fits the philosophy of Barcelona. He's a player who has done a great job at Liverpool – but maybe his work there is coming to an end.'

The feeling was that Owen would stay with the Reds if they qualified for another crack at the Champions League, but another season in the UEFA Cup would see the diminutive striker moving to pastures new. Such talk was very poorly received by the Liverpool fans, who felt Owen was holding the club to ransom and said as much at every opportunity, whether on radio phone-ins, websites or just down the pub.

As the new year started, the thoughts of the outspoken fans were the last of Owen's concerns, because football became entirely inconsequential when his long-term girlfriend, and the mother of his daughter fractured her pelvis in a horse riding accident. She also fractured a vertebra in two places and broke a finger.

Less than a week after Louise's fall, Owen made his long-awaited return from injury, starting the home win over Aston Villa. After such an extended absence he was expectedly short of his best, but everyone was disappointed when he failed to find the net in six consecutive starts.

With Owen firing blanks, the Reds were wallowing in fifth place in the Premiership, and a defeat at Tottenham and draws with Wolves, Everton and Bolton did little to improve their position behind Charlton. But, after three minutes of the game against Manchester City, Owen claimed his first goal for three and a half months, setting Liverpool on their way to a 2–1 win, and his good news didn't stop there.

On Valentine's Day the millionaire footballer proposed to his school sweetheart, and she said yes. It was also Louise's birthday. 'We are very happy together,' Owen announced.

Defeat against Portsmouth in the FA Cup left Liverpool with just the UEFA Cup and the Champions League place to concentrate on, but they couldn't find any solace in Europe, where they lost to Marseille in the last 16 of the UEFA Cup. A 1–0 win against Manchester United, followed by two wins and a draw, did see them clinch the fourth Champions League spot, but Liverpool had fallen well short of their expectations, 30 points behind Arsenal.

After such a poor campaign, finishing well off the title pace, and knocked out of all three cup competitions early, Liverpool would struggle to keep hold of their former

European Footballer of the Year. And talk of Owen's future once again filled the back pages.

'We'll sort something out this summer one way or another,' Owen said. 'It's never been about money but I want to win things. I've never wanted to be anything but successful and I know the manager shares that view.'

But, on 24 May, Gérard Houllier was sacked after six years at Liverpool, and the news filtered through to Owen on his pre-Euro 2004 training camp in Sardinia. Despite all that he had done for the club, it was time for Anfield's favourite Frenchman to move on. And he wasn't the only one.

12

Preparations for the Euro 2004 tournament in Portugal had been undermined by Chelsea's courting of Sven-Göran Eriksson, but the players were still bullish ahead of their trip to Portugal. 'I believe we will win it,' Owen said of the forthcoming tournament. 'We've played together a lot of times and have a lot of experience. We have some of the best players in the world, especially in the really important positions.'

England's start to the European Championship was highly anticipated by everyone in the footballing world: a showdown with holders France. Despite their failure at the last World Cup, Les Bleus were still rightfully considered one of the best teams in the world. And, with so many of their players earning a living in England, Owen and his teammates knew first-hand just how good their opponents were.

Eriksson's men exceeded expectations in their big game. They led for most of the match after Lampard headed home a Beckham free kick in the first half, but it was not to be their day and France won thanks to two late strikes from Zinédine Zidane.

Beckham even had a second-half penalty saved with the score at 1–0, but his Real Madrid teammate Zidane made no such mistake late on when an underhit backpass from Gerrard resulted in David James bringing down Thierry Henry for a penalty.

In the next game against Switzerland, Wayne Rooney announced his arrival as an international force with two goals in a 3–0 win. The first, after 23 minutes, made him the youngest player to score in European Championship finals, when he headed home Owen's cross; the second made the game safe with a quarter of an hour left to play. Gerrard added a late third but all the talk after the game was about Rooney's arrival and Owen's supposed demise.

Eriksson had replaced Owen with Vassell in the second half of the match but he dismissed allegations that the two Liverpudlians didn't work as a partnership. 'Wayne and Michael can play very good football together. I've no doubts about that. It's not a classic partnership with one tall and one small and quick, but they play well together.'

The much-sought-after goal failed to arrive for Owen in their final group match, but Rooney shone again with two more goals as England won 4–2 to secure progress in to the quarter-finals. 'Roomania' was gripping the footballing world and his strike partner still hadn't found the back of the net. 'It bothers me when I don't score,' the suddenly less-than-prolific Owen told the press. 'There's always something missing when you win a game and you haven't scored but, if you don't feel that way, then you'll never reach the top. Half of me is overjoyed that we're through to the quarter-finals but five per cent of me is disappointed I haven't scored.'

Facing the hosts in the Portuguese capital for a place in the semi-finals, Eriksson picked the same 11 for the third successive game, and England got off to the perfect start when Owen latched onto a defensive error to open the scoring after three minutes.

A nice early goal to settle the nerves should have enabled England to play to their potential, but the players seemed shackled by fear and few of them managed to play to their potential. The team also had to contend with bad luck when the inspirational Rooney was forced off with a broken foot with less than half an hour on the clock.

The team looked clueless without the teenager and they would soon be following their best player out of the Championship. Portugal found a way through with seven minutes left, and it was no less than they deserved. Hélder Postiga headed Simão's cross past James and the crowd went wild. There was still time for England to attack, though, and, when Owen headed Beckham's ninetieth-minute free kick against the bar, Campbell followed up to bundle the ball over the line. As the players began celebrating, the referee, Urs Meier, saw an alleged push by Terry on Ricardo and the game went into silver-goal extra time.

It was eerily similar to the game against Argentina at France '98, when Campbell had also had a last-minute 'goal' disallowed for a foul on the keeper. And, sadly for England, the end result would be the same.

The first half of the added thirty minutes was very nervy, as neither side was willing to commit too many men to any attack; but after 110 minutes of the match Rui Costa hit an unstoppable drive from outside the box into the top corner of James's net. With only ten minutes left, England had to attack, and five minutes from time they hit an equaliser, thanks to the Chelsea connection.

Terry nodded down a Beckham corner and Lampard was on hand to swivel on the edge of the six-yard box and smash the ball home. Despite missing crucial spot kicks against Turkey and France, Beckham was still England captain and he therefore put himself at the top of the list for the shootout.

As the skipper approached the ball his standing foot dislodged the ball, and when Beckham then struck it he got a horrible contact and sent his effort high over the bar. Owen took England's second penalty and scuffed it down the middle of the goal, because his leg cramped up as he shot, but he got away with it as the keeper dived out of the way anticipating an effort into the corner.

Successful spot kicks from Lampard, Terry and Hargreaves combined with one over the bar from Rui Costa, meaning that at 4–4 sudden-death penalties would be needed to settle the result. Ashley Cole put his away, but Vassell had his kick saved at 5–5. The Aston Villa striker's penalty was well struck and well placed, but Ricardo pulled off a brilliant save and then got up to score the deciding kick. England were knocked out of a fourth major tournament on penalties – and it hurt.

13

On 13 August 2004 Michael Owen left the club he had joined as an 11-year-old and joined Real Madrid. The biggest club in the world, the club with more European Cups than any other, Los Merengues, or as they have become better known in recent years, Los Galácticos.

Liverpool had brought in Rafa Benítez to replace Gérard Houllier, but the Spaniard couldn't persuade Owen to stay, and the England striker couldn't turn down the opportunity to join Real Madrid.

The fee was believed to be approximately £8 million, with midfielder Antonio Núñez moving to Anfield as a makeweight in the deal, and Owen was soon being unveiled to the press in Madrid. The Real Madrid president, Florentino Pérez, displayed his latest signing, saying, 'I hope Michael Owen will write a new page in the history of this club. We are signing an excellent player.'

Madrid certainly needed to start a new page, after finishing the previous season in fourth place in La Liga and without any silverware. Owen would contribute on the pitch, but his signing was also hoped to produce more revenue for Real in Asia, where Owen and his new teammate David Beckham had always been popular.

Owen wasn't interested in any of the marketing: he was just excited to get involved at his new club. 'It's a fantastic challenge for me,' he said. 'I'm impatient; I can't wait to put on the famous Real Madrid shirt. I've been to the Bernabéu in the past and now I realise it's the best stadium in the world and home to the best team in the world.'

Part of the presentation involved Owen's acceptance of his new No. 11 shirt. It was a good sign that Owen had received a nice low squad number, but there were no guarantees that he was going to be in the starting XI. 'I'm really looking forward to the challenge in front of me,' he went on. 'Raúl, Ronaldo and Fernando Morientes are three of the best strikers in the world – I'm aware of how hard I'm going to have to work to get an opportunity here.'

Owen made his Madrid debut against Real Mallorca, replacing Raul after 24 minutes, and created the only goal of the game for his Brazilian strike partner Ronaldo. He then returned to international duty to help England to a draw in Austria and a win in Poland as they got their World Cup qualifying campaign under way.

But there was no game time for Owen as Los Merengues got their Champions League campaign under way with a 3–0 defeat away to Bayer Leverkusen. It was an appalling result and, when it was followed by a 1–0 reverse away to Espanyol, head coach Camacho decided he'd had enough and he quit. It was not what Owen expected following his dream move to the biggest club in the world.

The England striker had made his first start in the game against Espanyol, but, as Camacho left, a new coach came in with new ideas and Madrid's No. 11 found himself back on the bench. When a second start finally came around Owen was forced to limp off after 52 minutes against Deportivo la Coruña with a thigh strain. The injury kept him out for only a couple of games, however, and he was fit again in time for England's next batch of World Cup qualifiers.

The first of these was one to relish for Owen, since it gave him an opportunity to shine against the country he had lived in for almost all his life. England beat Wales 2–0 at Old Trafford, Owen scoring with a deflection that was later credited to Lampard, but he had one of his own four days later, the only goal of the game, against Azerbaijan in the Tofik Bakhramov stadium.

Things on the pitch started improving for Owen after his return from international duty as he forced his way into the first XI and started five consecutive games for Madrid, and scored in the first four of them.

Unfortunately, Owen's streak came to an end, away in Kiev in the next game, and he was quickly restored to the role of bit-part player. He didn't even get consecutive starts for another month and a half, despite grabbing goals as a substitute against Malaga, Albacete and Levante.

Owen did have the honour of playing for his country at his club ground, as Spain entertained England in a friendly at the Bernabéu. But he lost bragging rights to his neighbours, because England lost 1–0. Los Merengues qualified for the last 16 of the Champions League by beating Roma 3–0 away, but they were still a little inconsistent in the league and would soon hire a third manager of the season.

While Owen was catching up with his old teammates

over Christmas, Real Madrid got rid of García Remón and replaced him with Vanderlei Luxemburgo. The former Brazil manager took control of Real Madrid over the Christmas break, and Owen didn't start two games in a row under his third manager of the season until the end of February. But Luxemburgo got off to a successful start with seven consecutive wins in La Liga, to close a 13-point gap on Barcelona to just four points, and he was forgiven his sparing use of Owen.

Despite his limited appearances, the England striker continued to score, and got goals from the bench against Real Zaragoza and Osasuna to help maintain the run. Owen also scored in the Copa del Rey, as Madrid were knocked out by second-division side Valladolid on away goals, and added to his England caps in the dour 0–0 friendly draw with Holland at Villa Park.

The lack of opportunity in Luxemburgo's team was clearly an irritation to Owen, who was shown by statistics in the Spanish newspapers to be the most lethal goalscorer in La Liga on account of his impressive goals-to-minutes-played ratio.

After scoring the winner against Osasuna, Owen was rewarded with his second league start under Luxemburgo, but Madrid's fine run came to an end with a 2–0 defeat at the hands of Athletic Bilbao. The players may have had one eye on their forthcoming Champions League clash with Juventus, and, although they beat the 'Old Lady of Turin' three days later 1–0 in the Bernabéu, Luxemburgo's team lost the second leg 2–0 in extra time in Italy to end their European campaign.

Owen was reduced to substitute appearances in both games, meaning his first season in Spain would end with only two Champions League starts for the most successful of all European teams. But he was working his way back into the side, and, in between the two games against Juventus, Owen had been chosen for his first consecutive starts of 2005, thanks to Raúl's bout of flu.

The former European Footballer of the Year had started talking more about a possible return to the Premiership, as he grew increasingly frustrated in La Liga. 'If I came home tomorrow, I would know that I have proved my abilities,' Owen said in *The Times*. 'I think about it a lot because I've got a lot of time to think over here and especially when I come back to meet up with England. Every time I join up, I feel I am coming back as a better, stronger player.'

Facing Northern Ireland in a World Cup qualifying game at Old Trafford, Owen scored his 29th goal for England as they won 4–0. But he was less impressive in the 2–0 victory against Azerbaijan that followed, and picked up a booking that ruled him out of the autumn clash with Wales.

'I can understand Gazza's tears in the 1990 World Cup semi-final.' He said. 'To miss a qualifying game in Cardiff might not seem as important but, for me, it was shaping up as one of the biggest matches of the year. I will not be playing any cup finals with Real Madrid and it's not looking too pretty for us in the Spanish league, so a trip to a packed Millennium Stadium was something to relish.'

Things improved on the pitch at Madrid, however, as Owen started the last nine games of the season. He scored the winning goal at Albacete, filling in for a sick Raúl, and got another, far more important goal a week later as Madrid beat Barcelona 4–2 at the Bernabéu, closing the gap at the top of the table to six points with seven games left.

It was the kind of night that had motivated Owen's move to the world's most famous club, and he received a well-deserved standing ovation when Luis Figo replaced him with ten minutes remaining.

Luxemburgo didn't dare to drop Owen after a win over the Catalan side, and nor should he have done so. Indeed, the Englishman's stock had risen to such an extent that he wasn't even dropped when he didn't score in the wins over Levante, Villareal and Real Sociedad. But the team were working, and they made it six wins in a row with Owen among their number, as they beat Racing Santander 5–0, with the Englishman grabbing one. But Barca were also winning, and Madrid's fading hopes of the title evaporated completely when they drew their next game away to Sevilla.

Having seen the title slip away, Real failed to lift themselves for the Madrid derby against Atletico, and drew 0–0, before closing the curtain on the campaign with a 3–1 win over Real Zaragoza. Owen scored the opening goal, before being replaced at the interval by Luis Figo, as the manager gave the Portuguese midfielder a last 45 minutes in a Real Madrid shirt.

In his first year in Spain, Owen had endured some tough times, but had ridden them out. And, by starting the last nine games and scoring four goals in the process, he had moved to 13 league goals for the season.

The striker claimed 16 in total for Madrid, helping the club to finish the season on 80 points, second to Barcelona by four points, and he had fired England to within touching distance of the 2006 World Cup.

14

Speculation continued about Owen's future. Having left Liverpool to play at the highest level and win silverware, Owen was asked about watching his former teammates come back from 3–0 down at half-time to beat AC Milan on penalties and win the Champions League. Despite finishing the season trophyless in Spain, he said he had no regrets and was happy for Liverpool. 'It was fantastic,' he said.

Owen took advantage of a rare summer without a tournament and finally married his long-term girlfriend Louise Bonsall. The pair married at the Carden Park Hotel near Chester in a very private ceremony in front of a dozen relatives and close friends in June 2005. But they also celebrated their vows with a huge party at their house, and sold the picture rights to *Hello!* magazine. The happy couple enjoyed a fabulous honeymoon before Owen returned to football – and a third club, Newcastle United.

The summer had been spent in limbo, with various voices from the Madrid hierarchy stating unequivocally that Owen was staying, while the press continued to speculate on his likely destinations. After the Brazilian duo Robinho and Júlio Baptista signed for Real, it became apparent that Owen was no longer wanted at the Bernabéu.

With the World Cup only 10 months away, there was no chance of Owen staying at a club where he would be fourth- or fifth-choice striker, and it was time for him to head home to England. He was linked with Chelsea, Arsenal, Manchester United and Liverpool before Newcastle United sealed the deal, pairing Owen with his old England ally Shearer once again.

Souness compared his new signing to that which brought Shearer home nine years previously. 'He's someone who can become a legend with Newcastle United fans,' the Newcastle manager said of Owen. 'In football, the hardest thing to get in your team is someone who puts the ball in the back of the net, and Michael is the best at doing that. I can understand people who liken it to the signing of Alan Shearer. I'd say it's the biggest transfer I've been involved in as a manager of any football club.'

Owen signed a four-year deal worth an estimated £80,000 per week, and there were 20,000 Geordie fans at St James' Park to see him presented with his new black and white No. 10 shirt. He was joined by a number of other signings as Newcastle looked to build on their disappointing bottom-half finish in 2004-05: Scott Parker, Albert Luque, Nolberto Solano and Emre Belözoglu.

Having watched England beat Wales 1–0 in Cardiff, Owen returned to international duty in a humiliating 1–0 defeat to Northern Ireland. 'It was a disappointing result but at least I'm playing,' said Owen.

Two weeks later, he scored the second of Newcastle's

three goals in a win at Blackburn. It was the first victory of the season for the Magpies and brought three much-needed points to ease the pressure on Souness.

Owen made it two from two the following week, to get his first home goal for Newcastle and secure a second win of the season, as Manchester City were beaten 1–0. 'We're on a roll and I'm delighted with the win,' he said. 'It was a special feeling to have people calling my name after I scored, especially so loudly.'

Owen's latest hot streak was cut short by a leg injury picked up in training, and he was forced out of the 0–0 draw at Portsmouth, but it wasn't serious enough to keep him out of England's last two World Cup qualifiers, where six points would guarantee their place in Germany the following summer. Owen failed to score against a managerless Austrian side, but a 1–0 win at Old Trafford and other results that went their way meant that Eriksson's team qualified for the World Cup. With 22 points from their nine games, England were guaranteed a place in the finals as the best group runner-up, even if they lost to Poland. But there was to be no easing up from the England squad and they got a second win in Manchester, 2–1, with goals from Owen, who was captain once again in the absence of the suspended Beckham and Frank Lampard, leaving them top of Group 6.

The Newcastle striker was now joint level with Gary Lineker, having scored 22 competitive goals for England, and his thoughts were already turning to Germany the following summer. 'We should be optimistic,' he said. 'When you get to a World Cup you need players you can look at and think, "He can win a game on his own." We've got the likes of Frank Lampard and Steven Gerrard. If just one puts in a fantastic performance in a game, that could get us through maybe to the semi-finals.

'Then you look around and see a Wayne Rooney and other players and think, "If he can turn it on, that bit of magic might open up another top team." The more top players you've got, the more chance you've got of creating a bit of skill and magic – and Wayne is definitely one of those sorts of people.'

Owen had settled in to the northeast quickly, and his off-field happiness was evident in his on-pitch displays. 'My daughter Gemma's not shown any signs of a Geordie accent yet, but it's only a matter of time!' he told the press with a smile. 'But our second baby's due in February and we've put roots down here.'

Newcastle had been good for Owen and he had been good for them, helping them to 14 points from seven games, and they made it 17 from eight with a 1–0 home win over Birmingham, before a groin strain put him out of action for a month. The Magpies' form suffered without their record signing and they crashed out of the Carling Cup and dropped eight points from three league games.

Owen had played eight games, scoring seven goals, and helped his new team to 19 points from a possible 24. In the games the England man had missed since signing, the Magpies had picked up five points from a possible 15. And Shearer was quite rightly delighted with his new strike partner. 'He really is the difference between our being an average side and a very good side,' the former England captain told the press.

Unfortunately, that partnership wasn't able to develop, because Owen's season was effectively over within a fortnight, but not before the former Liverpool striker made an emotional return to Anfield. 'It's hard for me to know what it's going to be like until the game,' Owen told the *Liverpool Echo* before the game. 'There are lots of things I've thought about. What do I do if I score? What do I do if Carra gives me a kick up the backside? These aren't things I'll know how to react to until it happens. I'm going to be playing against people who are my best friends.'

He didn't have to worry about goal celebrations as Newcastle were beaten 2–0, but more disappointing for Owen was the reaction of the Kop, who jeered his every touch and abused him with chants throughout the game. 'You should have signed for a big club' was one of their favourites; 'What a waste of talent!' kept them mildly entertained; while, 'Where were you in Istanbul?' seemed a bit of a low blow.

As low as Owen might have felt after his miserable return to Anfield, he would have felt a lot worse five days later, when he broke the fifth metatarsal in his right foot in a collision with his England teammate, Tottenham goalkeeper Paul Robinson. It was terrible news for Newcastle, who lost the game at White Hart Lane 2–0, after Owen hobbled off, and Souness was sacked little more than a month later. But from an England perspective, at least he had time to recover before the World Cup.

He celebrated the birth of his second child, James Michael, on 6 February 2006. Owen was especially delighted by the birth of his first son, and he was keen for James to extend the footballing Owens to a third generation. 'People have asked me if I'd like him to be a footballer, and of course I would,' the happy father said.

Owen made his comeback for Newcastle under caretaker-manager Glenn Roeder in the Magpies' penultimate league match, playing the final 30 minutes as a substitute, but walked very gingerly away from the ground. Fortunately, there was no further damage to the foot, but a first game back had taken its toll and Owen didn't appear for the final game of the season at home to Chelsea.

In Owen's first season for Newcastle he had shown he still had his knack for scoring goals, as his seven from 10 starts showed, but after his injury the Magpies had cruised through the rest of the campaign to finish seventh in the league, and he was looking forward to getting them further up the table when he returned to fitness – but no one could have predicted how long he would have to wait for that opportunity.

After entering the World Cup unfit after his broken foot, the Newcastle striker left it with a career-threatening knee injury. With Rooney having broken a metatarsal as well, and facing a much more desperate race to get fit in time for the tournament, there was concern that the pressure on the Newcastle striker would be too much for him in the wake of his own injury. Indeed, Owen still looked a little rusty in the England's first group match against Paraguay, and was replaced by Stewart Downing after 55 minutes. The England team weren't at their best either and relied on an own goal to win the game, as Beckham's third-minute free kick was headed home by defender Carlos Gamarra.

Owen failed to score against Trinidad and Tobago too, and was replaced after 58 minutes as Rooney made his World Cup debut from the bench. Goals from Crouch and Gerrard helped England to win 2–0, and there was the suggestion that Owen might start the final Group B match

on the bench. 'I'm not worried,' Owen said ahead of the Sweden clash. 'If I'm sat on the bench, I'm sat on the bench. I've been on the bench in my career before.'

Owen did start against Sweden, but lasted less than a minute. He ruptured the anterior cruciate ligament (one of the four major ligaments) in his right knee and as England drew 2–2 to finish top of the group and secure the easier second-round match, against Ecuador, Owen's World Cup was over.

England managed to squeeze past Ecuador 1–0 without Owen, but they came unstuck against Portugal in the quarter-finals after Rooney was sent off, and they lost on penalties. It was another disappointing tournament for England's quality players, but once again the manager had failed to produce a team of more than the sum of the parts at his disposal, and another trophy chance went begging for the Three Lions.

After picking up his second serious injury in the last seven months, Owen could have been forgiven for feeling sorry for himself, but he was just sorry for the Toon Army, who wouldn't see him play again before 2007.

15

When Michael Owen returned injured from the World Cup to face a serious operation on his knee, it heralded the start of probably the most frustrating years of his career. In typical Owen style, he remained bullish, insisting he had no doubts he would be back fit and scoring goals in record time. But in many ways the injury proved to be the least of Owen's concerns as Newcastle lurched from one disaster to another and England's fortunes followed a similar pattern.

The first hint of what was in store arrived almost as soon as Owen's flight touched down and he found himself at the centre of a club versus country row. Newcastle were furious at the prospect of being without their star player for such a long period, particularly as he had been injured not while wearing the black and white of his paymasters but while playing for his country.

The club demanded serious compensation from the FA, with some reports suggesting they wanted as much as £20m to cover his wages, lost revenue and the cost of buying in a replacement – £10m striker Obafemi Martins.

There were even suggestions Newcastle could take out an injunction preventing the FA from selecting Owen in future England squads, although such claims had a ring of tabloid sensationalism about them. But there is no doubt the row was a fierce one, with FIFA eventually introducing a compensation fund for injuries sustained at World Cups in a bid to prevent it happening again.

By the time Owen began training again for the first time, in February 2007, the row was in full flow and it took until the summer to sort it, with The FA eventually agreeing a revised payment of between £7m and £10m.

On the pitch, Owen made his comeback on 10 April in a behind-closed-doors friendly against Gretna and, of course, scored in the process. But although he played his first full game for Newcastle in over a year later that month, against Reading in a 1–0 defeat, the trauma was not yet over.

His injury nightmare struck again at the end of the season when he was carried off on a stretcher after colliding with team-mate Matty Pattison in a match against Watford. It was only concussion but with reports rife that Owen could be set to leave Newcastle at the end of the campaign, it was not the image the striker wanted fans to remember.

Life at Newcastle was far from rosy. Manager Glenn Roeder resigned in May 2007 after being summoned to a board meeting following the team's dismal run of just one win in 10 games, leaving Nigel Pearson to take control for the final weeks of the campaign as fans protested against the board.

The arrival of Sam Allardyce as Newcastle's new manager didn't help either, as his efforts to shore up a notoriously leaky defence resulted in a style of play that was not appreciated by the Toon Army, and new owner Mike Ashley appeared to be swayed by their opinion.

When Newcastle, sitting 11th in the Premiership, produced a miserable display to draw 0–0 against Championship side Stoke in the FA Cup – a match they were fortunate not to lose – the axe finally fell. On Wednesday 9 January 2008, Allardyce left the club 'by mutual consent'.

After a frenzy of speculation as to who would replace him, Ashley offered the job to Harry Redknapp, only for him to turn it down. There seemed to be only one solution – and Ashley produced what at the time seemed a masterstroke by persuading the Messiah, Kevin Keegan, to return to the club.

Fans flocked to St James' Park to welcome the Messiah back and there was talk of a new era on Tyneside and a return to the glory days of exciting football and European nights under the lights. Just for a second it seemed possible, too, with Owen scoring in a 4–1 FA Cup replay demolition of Stoke City in January 2008 as Keegan watched from the stands.

The striker was also handed the captain's armband by Keegan and although it took until March for Newcastle to win their first league match under Special K, Owen scoring in a 2–0 victory over Fulham, the atmosphere had certainly been lifted.

It looked good for Owen, too, because despite all the injury problems he ended the season with 11 goals and, at last, seemed at home in the black and white shirt.

Somehow, however, they managed to stuff it all up.

The following season began promisingly enough with a 1–1 draw at Manchester United, a 1–0 victory over Bolton courtesy of an Owen header and a 3–2 extra-time Carling Cup victory at Coventry in which Owen also found the net.

But something wasn't quite right between Keegan and his employers and the tensions at board level would eventually hit melting point as the big-money signings everyone expected failed to materialise.

Keegan left on 2 September, just hours after the closure of the transfer window, and even intensive talks with Ashley could not resolve the issue. Keegan later sued the club, successfully, for unfair dismissal.

Owen must have despaired at the situation, which also saw Mike Ashley offer the club for sale and then take it off the market in the space of the next few months. Little wonder, then, that in December 2008, Owen rejected the offer of a new contract and insisted he would look for a new club at the end of the season. With Newcastle in dangerous water in the Premiership, he promised he would not bail out in January and would stay to fight relegation, eventually contributing 10 goals for the campaign. But it proved to be a thankless task.

Stand-in manager Joe Kinnear underwent heart surgery in February 2009, leaving assistant Chris Hughton in temporary charge of the team. And then, in a desperate bid to save the season, Ashley appointed fans' favourite Alan Shearer as manager for the final eight games of the campaign. But it wasn't enough to save the Toon from the drop – their fate was sealed by a 1–0 defeat at Aston Villa on the final day of the season.

Those three tough years on Tyneside since the 2006

World Cup had virtually destroyed Owen's England career. Injury ruled him out of the opening six qualifiers for Euro 2008 but he returned to score against Estonia and break Gary Lineker's record for the most goals in competitive England internationals – 26.

He also scored twice in the 3–0 victory over Russia in September 2007, which seemed to pave the way for England to reach the finals in Austria and Switzerland. But the qualifying tournament ended in disaster as England lost 4–2 at home to Croatia and missed out on a place in the finals. Manager Steve McClaren was sacked the very next day and Owen has barely had a look-in since.

The arrival of Fabio Capello as manager has seen the striker largely ignored, currently stuck on 40 goals and 89 caps, just nine goals short of all-time record holder Bobby Charlton. It's inevitable that some people will conclude that Owen's time at Newcastle had a serious effect on his reputation.

'I know my reputation as a footballer and as a professional suffered at Newcastle,' Owen admitted in an interview in the *Guardian* newspaper. 'I'd never try to shirk my share of the blame for the club being relegated. I played 33 games last season and I know I could have done a lot better.

'But some of the criticism that was levelled at me was bordering on the ridiculous. I played 33 and 32 games in the last two years in a Newcastle team that was not in Europe and did not go on a decent cup run. Still I was continually labelled injury-prone, which gets up my nose. I am 29 and have played over 500 games for club and country. That says it all.'

Fortunately for Owen, he wasn't the only person thinking that way. And just as one door was closing, another very attractive one was about to open...

16

Manchester United's number seven shirt has always been one of the most glamorous and prestigious in the history of European football. Think George Best, think Bryan Robson, think Cristiano Ronaldo.

So when Ronaldo, the man who inspired United to Champions League glory in 2008 and to three Premier League titles in a row, finally left Old Trafford for life at Real Madrid in the summer of 2009, manager Sir Alex Ferguson had a dilemma.

Where on earth do you turn to fill the boots and shirt of a legend?

The answer, provided at a packed press conference on 3 July 2009, shocked everyone. The answer was Michael Owen.

When you analyse it, the decision was certainly a brave one. After all, Owen doesn't share the same sublime skills as Ronaldo and Best on the pitch and certainly not their love of the high life off it – unless you put training racehorses in the same bracket as dating Miss Worlds and wearing skimpy shorts in calendar shoots!

But, as the glossy 32-page brochure put together by Owen's agents in a bid to find him a new club highlighted, he is a superstar in his own right and a man with huge experience at the very highest level in the game. The fact that he was available on a free transfer from Newcastle appealed to frugal Fergie, too, of course. But what he was really signing was guaranteed goals and true world-class stature.

And that's why Ferguson is adamant his number seven will help fans forget about the old one.

'Michael gives us experience in the penalty box, which is vital,' the Scotsman said after Owen agreed terms. 'He has always had that little knack of losing defenders in the last third. I know he will score a lot of goals for us. He has been great at that for years.'

Owen signed a two-year contract at Old Trafford and it quickly became clear that Ferguson, who also tried to sign him as a teenager but was beaten to his signature by Liverpool, had immense faith in his new arrival – especially after handing him that number seven shirt. The only question now is: can Owen live up to that billing, guide United to further glory and take his own career to a new level? In short, can he live up to the shirt?

Not surprisingly, the answer from the England star so far has been a resounding 'yes'. 'When United came in for me I thought about the players I'd be alongside, playing at Old Trafford in a team that you know will create chances. Then I went to bed and when I woke up the next morning it really hit me. I thought, "Hell, I can win a league title here and play in the Champions League." Let's just say that I am very excited!'

Owen's first competitive goal for United came against Wigan in a 5–0 victory for Fergusons's champions. But it was his first home goal that really made the headlines. That's because it came against deadly rivals Manchester City in the very last minute of injury time – and earned United a stunning 4–3 derby day victory.

That goal means Owen has now scored in four different derby fixtures – for Liverpool against Everton, for Real Madrid against Barcelona, for Newcastle against Sunderland and now for United against City.

And, more importantly, of course, it finally ended any suggestion that United fans were reluctant to take him to their hearts because of his Anfield past.

'The reception for me has been great,' he later told Sky in a television interview. 'Although I must admit when I first signed it was one of the things I thought, "What type of reaction will I get?" But they've been absolutely fine, there's been no problem whatsoever.'

Owen has since played for United against Liverpool at Anfield and even if that match ended in a disappointing 2–0 defeat the question of his commitment to Manchester is unlikely to be raised again.

With United challenging on all fronts as usual, the only question mark that remained concerned his ability to force his way into the England squad and end the season not only as a trophy winner with his club but as a World Cup star for his country.

Logic said that if Owen was playing for United at the highest level and scoring goals then he would be almost impossible to ignore once the squad for South Africa was decided in May 2010. But unfortunately, as has been the case so many times over Michael Owen's career, there was a lot more to it than that.

England manager Fabio Capello hadn't selected Owen for an England squad since his second match in charge, an away friendly against France in Paris in January 2008 and seemed, at best, reluctant to rock the boat by changing his policy.

Owen's rivals for the shirt – players such as Jermain Defoe, Peter Crouch and Carlton Cole, had all been scoring and playing regularly in the Premiership and had consistently been selected ahead of him. More than that, Capello seemed irritated and uncomfortable when asked about Owen's future chances and stuck rigidly to an insistence that the striker had not played enough games and is not fit enough to risk.

Owen steadfastly refused to criticise Capello's decision to leave him out and instead insisted he would be ready if and when he got the call.

'I have just got to continue doing well and see where that will take me,' he said. 'I have been in the provisional squad quite a few times, though the final squad is the one you want to be in.'

Somewhat prophetically, he continued: 'It's good to see England doing so well but unfortunately every time the squad comes around I seem to have picked up a small injury even though I'm back to fitness now. Or maybe at Newcastle at times I was a bit out of form.

'There are no excuses for me. Obviously now I need to play really well for my club and score a few goals and

hopefully get back in it. I have always been optimistic about that.

'I haven't changed as a player – I'll always score goals. I've got a record to show that. I think everyone knows what they will get from me and I've proved it in World Cups before.

'But the last thing I want to do is start a Michael Owen for England campaign and say all the reasons why I could or should be selected. I'm at ease with myself and the situation and I know what I've got to do and that's to play well for Manchester United.

'I've not spoken to Fabio Capello about it and I don't need to – I know the situation, I need to play well and score goals and do well for United and then I could get picked. But as I say I'm at ease with it. I don't lie awake at night thinking this or that. It's a simple enough equation – play well and you'll be in and don't and you won't.

'As I say, I have had a letter every time to be in the preliminary squad. I know from being in those squads that the manager, Fabio Capello, is keeping an eye on me. I am confident I will play for England.

'To get into that squad and go to the World Cup is the ultimate aim for every English footballer, but that's not until the summer. I still have time to do as well as possible.'

Sadly, Owen didn't get that seat on the plane to South Africa. Yet another injury was to blame – a seemingly innocuous hamstring problem sustained during United's Carling Cup final victory over Aston Villa on 28 February turned out to be more serious than first thought, ruling him out for the rest of the season and putting paid to his dreams of England glory. But it's easy to forget amid all the fuss about his injuries that he is still only 29 years old and in his prime. So let's hope he bounces back, as he has done so many times in the past. His career is certainly not over, and he could yet have his fairytale ending.